abroad, courtesy of her father's job in the Foreign Office.

After completing her A-Levels, she went to Nottingham University to take an American Studies degree and then joined a prominent bank's graduate training programme. She stayed in banking for ten years before having her three children.

Alli later went on to work as a gardener before running a bed and breakfast in the Midlands with her husband.

This is her first published book and she now divides her time writing with being a domestic goddess.

Life's a Bag of Laughs

Alli Rogers

Life's a Bag of Laughs

Vanguard Press

VANGUARD PAPERBACK

© Copyright 2014
Alli Rogers

A CIP catalogue record for this title is
available from the British Library.

ISBN 978 1 84386 985 6

Author photo reproduced with kind permission from
Dawn Branigan Photography
www.shotatdawn.com
dawn@shotatdawn.com

Vanguard Press is an imprint of
Pegasus Elliot MacKenzie Publishers Ltd.
www.pegasuspublishers.com

First Published in 2014

Vanguard Press
Sheraton House Castle Park
Cambridge England

Printed & Bound in Great Britain

This is for Debbie to say a big thank you for the New Zealand trip and your unwitting contribution to my book.

We haven't seen much of each other over the years but I think you know me well. Well enough to forgive my off-beat sense of humour. Enjoy!

P.S Please say thanks to the Tui.

Contents

CHAPTER 1

A BAG OF LAUGHS

"Do you want a bag?"

A bored, robotic voice interrupted my 'to do list' thoughts.

Well, yes, I *did* need a bag – pretty obvious really, as I was only clutching a small bumbag and my wire chemist's basket was full. So unless the girl behind the counter thought I was some closet kangaroo with a handy pouch, (oh so convenient for those many purchases) then a bag was a definite must.

A sarcastic response rose to my lips but was suppressed with a sigh of resignation. Good old-fashioned customer service seems to have evaporated, subjected as we are to an obsessive bag culture. No "Good morning" or "Hello" – just a determination to ascertain one's bag requirements ASAP.

Now, don't get me wrong. I'm all for saving the planet and doing my bit. I consider myself to be an avid recycler at home. However, I do object to being made to feel guilty for having the audacity to request or need a bag. It's got to the point where I fear the Bag Police may sneak up on me one day.

"Excuse me, is that bag really necessary, madam?"

"Oh well, yes, officer... I... I..."

You get my drift.

I don't know why the retailers don't just provide robust paper bags. Easy to recycle and kinder to the planet. Then we might all be allowed a bag without the suggestion that we have committed some heinous crime. It's not as if people go around asking for extra bags over and above their needs for a bit of a laugh. No doubt there will soon be a law to stop such profligate bag requests. Guilty of the crime of inappropriately procuring a bag under false pretences. I rest my case.

So why did I have bag rage on that particular day? Simple. I had just returned from visiting my sister Debbie in New Zealand, where in every shop, without fail, I was met with a cheery greeting and no miserable old bag asked me if I wanted a bag. Great!

I admit I am no handbag lady — never been one for bags, although to be fair, I do own two decent ones but sadly lacking in designer kudos. It never ceases to amaze me what women are prepared to pay for a bag or indeed how anyone could need so many. It must be a full-time job for some, keeping up with the latest trends — big ones, small ones... Posh should know! Posh (aka Mrs David Beckham) surely is to bags what Imelda Marcos was to shoes. Still we all have our vices and I confess I have a distinct weakness for boots. However, I suspect I will never suffer bag envy. Give me my bumbag any day, even if I can't fit a week's shopping in it.

Anyway, after my disgruntled bag debacle, I made my weary jet-lagged way home, wondering how on earth I could possibly have needed to visit a chemist again this decade, having purchased every lotion, potion, and drug known to man prior to my departure for New Zealand.

CHAPTER 2

MY FRIEND THRUSH

Over the years I have travelled a lot and, having reached the SAGA milestone of fifty, with age comes wisdom. I now go armed with vast supplies of 'just in case' medication; my theory being, if you have the remedy to hand the symptoms will never appear. A strange psychology perhaps, but it does work.

Take for example *Thrush* – and *no*, I don't mean the feathered variety. I refer to that elusive itch – the itch you can't scratch. The bane of women's lives. For you ladies lucky enough to have 'escaped' the pleasure of this irritating gynaecological problem, that has the habit of presenting at the most inconvenient of times, lucky you! I say inconvenient but come to think of it, when is it convenient to have a bout of *Thrush*? Try never and you'll be getting close.

In my experience, it has the nasty habit of sneaking up on you when you are on holiday abroad. Let's face it, who wants to try explaining to a foreign chemist in sign language what your problem is? Pointing at your pubic area and scratching in mid air can be very embarrassing and not one of your finest moments.

During one holiday to Gran Canaria, I felt positively smug at having eluded the *Thrush* curse for the duration. Of course how was I to know that I would be blessed with a dreadful case of piles instead? Yes, back to pointing at nether regions again at some bemused chemist. No laughing matter.

And neither is the issue of cost. Do you realise how expensive it is to keep treating recurring *Thrush*? I could have paid off the third world debt if I hadn't ploughed a fortune into those magic remedies or at least paid for a flight to New Zealand. There have been times when I have felt compelled to give my bank account details to the drug companies with *carte blanche* to help themselves to my money. Dare I say you have little choice but to accept they have you by the short and curlies and pay!

You may detect that I have become a little cynical and jaded over the years and have decided that a temporary cure for my predicament will not suffice. Prevention, not cure has become the new mantra of life.

You are probably aware of the triggers – tight jeans for example – pity because I prefer tight jeans. Wear cotton pants. I do. Don't bathe indulgently in bubble bath or use excessive soap. I don't. But I am not easily thwarted.

My GP, whom I have wearily sat opposite explaining my woes has nodded unsympathetically and muttered that some women are just unlucky (indeed) and prone to the *Thrush* virus. Not a very helpful attitude and lacking in the prevention approach.

I once thought that a certain play gel was exacerbating the problem, so armed with this 'medical discovery' I shared my new found suspicions with another GP. Interest hardly registered on the Richter scale and I was definitely not

nominated for an acknowledgement in the *Lancet* medical journal. Back to square one.

However, on one occasion, having tried all the usual over-the-counter remedies with limited success, my GP raised my hopes by prescribing a different cream. I left the surgery with glee at the prospect of a 'eureka, I'm cured' moment. OMG! BIG mistake on my behalf.

If I said that after applying said cream my 'bits' felt like they had been dipped in acid, I would not be exaggerating. Bring back the *Thrush*! All is forgiven! Needless to say that particular medication was quickly consigned to the bin.

On a more positive note, *Thrush* does instigate a sense of camaraderie amongst we ladies. If you ever hear someone bemoan the *Thrush* curse, there is always a cacophony of muttered sympathy from fellow sufferers. For those lucky enough not to be privy to the experience (my teenage daughter Jocelyn has eluded it – how, I ask you?) I shall declare myself peeved and not a little jealous.

Strangely, of late my pre-disposition to *Thrush* has improved dramatically for no rhyme or reason, change in life style or habit. If indeed my 'friend' has packed its bags and left me for pastures new, bring it on.

CHAPTER 3

OMG

Talking of bags, my case and hand luggage were still lurking at home as I returned from my chemist trip, only half unpacked, two days after getting back from New Zealand. This general tardiness is totally out of character for me. However, jet lag, following a thirty-eight hour door-to-door journey had left me wiped out and feeling like I had been jumped on by a giant kangaroo and jumped on again, just for good measure. And if this analogy does not ring a bell with you, be grateful that it doesn't.

Despite having suffered no ill effects on my journey out and displaying unexpected amounts of energy on my arrival, I certainly succumbed on the return journey. Not surprising really when you consider the implications of a long haul flight. There is little to recommend it (especially if you are travelling economy) even if you are lured by your final destination. At least on the way out the excitement of the holiday beckons. As for the return journey, you can always rely on the captain's parting words regarding the British weather to dampen your spirits. You can't beat a bit of 'welcome home hypothermia' before you've even reached passport control.

I think most people can cope with the flight itself even if there are a few children on board devoid of volume control. It's all the getting to the airport, waiting about and refuelling stop-overs that leave you half-dead. Not to mention ample opportunity to get bored long before take-off. Unless you are riveted by perfume shops, in ecstasies at the prospect of thumbing through potential reading matter in the bookshops and oblivious to the inflated drinks and food prices. Of course you could while your time away trying on endless pairs of designer sunglasses – anything to avoid sitting. After all, you can virtually guarantee the acquisition of a flat, numb bum on the plane.

The prospect of a long, tedious flight was made all the more daunting as I was travelling alone. I confess I was also filled with trepidation at the thought of seeing my second eldest sister. Why? Because I had not seen her in seven years and contact with her had been sporadic verging on non-existent. Not that we had ever fallen out or had cause for animosity. So you can imagine my surprise when one Sunday evening, tucked up on the sofa with a glass of wine and a post roast dinner tummy my mobile rang and an international number flashed up. It was Debbie. Rather bizarrely she declared she was changing her will partly in my favour having lost humour with her errant thirty-two-year-old daughter who lives in America. Not only that but she offered to pay for my flight to see her. Quite a surreal moment.

So that is how I found myself flying to New Zealand leaving my three children with their father. My parents were delighted that Debbie was in touch again. My eldest sister Gill was incredulous.

Now travelling alone without a partner or friend to chat to can be quite a lonely experience, so what can you do but resort to people watching? Now, you have to admit this can be quite compelling.

As I waited in the departure lounge in Manchester airport, I had a major OMG moment. Sat opposite me was the most enormous man and I *do* mean enormous. My first thought was how could he feasibly squeeze into a standard plane seat, but this conundrum was quickly replaced by my panic that he could be sitting next to me. The prospect of being incarcerated in a small seat for endless hours with the inevitable likelihood that your space would be encroached on was not appealing. I tried to assure myself that perhaps he had booked two seats or was in business or first class where seats are more suitable for larger brethren. And to think that I had worried my suitcase was a couple of kilos overweight. I assume airlines don't charge for overweight people, just overweight bags. As I only weigh eight stone ten pounds, perhaps I could put a valid argument for a greater luggage allowance in future. In any event, my panic was unfounded as my space issues did not come to fruition.

Instead, I had the undoubted pleasure of sitting next to two obnoxious children and their sycophantic, over indulgent parents. Oh joy. And just for the icing on the cake, I had some little treasure behind me who was a consummate seat kicker. Thinking matters could not get any worse, shortly after take-off, two babies serenaded the plane with their co-ordinated screeching. Bliss!

Luckily, I had come armed with ear plugs, although, even they were challenged. All was not lost however, as the flight crew were exceptionally polite, cheerful and accommodating. I marvelled at their constant patience and humour especially their amazing skill for fitting passengers' over-sized hand-luggage into Tardis-like lockers. I must admit that I wished a few of the less desirable on-board could be placed in the over-head lockers for the duration of the flight, on more than one occasion.

Especially one particular child who screamed in petulant self indulgent rage at his long suffering parents that he 'didn't want to' and 'no way' for more air miles than I care to remember. At one point I was thinking if DVT didn't get me, insanity would. Thank heavens he disembarked at Singapore where the plane stopped to refuel.

CHAPTER 4

BAG A BARGAIN

My father had declared prior to my departure how "exciting" it was that I should be going to Singapore, having been born there. Well, not *that* exciting – after all, it was only the airport I was seeing. I did the usual to kill time, wandering into all the duty-free shops, even the exclusive handbag outlets, where I peered at bags and bags of you guessed it... bags. As most of them were worth more than my car, I confess it felt a little incongruous eying up such designer fare clutching my bumbag!

As for the suitcases and the eye-watering price tags, I wondered if the shop had any loan deals available over twenty years to facilitate such a purchase. Now, I *do* own a couple of decent suitcases but one in particular, acquired under duress in France about eight years ago comes to mind. I was flying with a certain budget airline with my husband James and our three children, going to the South of France in search of French cuisine, culture, wine, sun and relaxation but definitely not suitcases.

I am now wiser after said acquisition and avoid cheap flights at all cost. They appear cheap at first sight and one is lured and tempted into a false bargain. But by the time you have been charged for every conceivable extra, including the air you may breathe on-board and been asked to flap your arms to facilitate take-off, you realise you have been ripped off.

Whilst waiting in the queue to book in our luggage, we noticed a lot of frantic case opening and repacking going on around us. It transpired that passengers' suitcases were not the acceptable weight. When our turn came, despite the fact that we were well within our luggage allowance (having booked and paid for three suitcases but actually only arriving with two to facilitate travel) our cases were deemed to be overweight and we were charged a huge penalty. So in order to avoid incurring the same penalty on the return journey, we had no choice but to buy another case whilst on holiday. We dutifully purchased a worryingly expensive suitcase in the beautiful town of Bezier and to this day, it has been known as the Bezier Bag.

CHAPTER 5

FLOAT MY BOAT

To while my long journey to New Zealand away, I had packed two books – the first unread and the second, a nostalgic memory trip for me and my all-time favourite book – *The Hobbit*.

I first read this book when I was eleven years old. I was on a cruise ship with my parents, travelling from Sydney, Australia, back to England after my father's two-and-a-half-year tour in Darwin with The Foreign Office had ended in 1974.

To say that Bilbo Baggins of Bag End and his adventures with Gandalf and the dwarves captivated me would be an understatement. Just as well really as I suffered the most hideous *Gastroenteritis* and chronic seasickness for six weeks and was virtually bed-ridden, during which time I read the book thirteen times! As the book has recently come to the public attention again with the movie being made and coincidentally filmed in New Zealand, it seemed apt to visit my literary yesterday.

As I was so poorly on the cruise and able to keep precious little down, I survived on a frugal diet of Edam cheese, apples and the odd bag of crisps. To this day, I cannot stand the sight or taste of Edam cheese and a few years ago acquired a bizarre allergy to raw apples. As for crisps, I confess to having a certain weakness for them despite the fact that my mother entered me into the ship's fancy dress competition dressed as a bag of crisps; the outfit being made of crepe paper and fashioned by her determined hands. She was adamant that I would win the competition, despite my protestations and under no circumstance was I to be sick. Unfortunately I was unable to oblige but luckily a photo was taken just in time to record the event.

It was not the first time I had been subjected to such humiliation. When I was six years old in 1968, I was travelling on another cruise ship going to Uganda where my father was due to start work at the High Commission in Kampala. Another fancy dress competition loomed and this time my mother decided to send me as a ballroom dancer from *The Black and White Minstrel Show*. For those of you too young to remember, this was a light entertainment programme with the male dancers blacking up their faces, prancing about with pretty women in glamorous dresses. Certainly not very politically correct – and even in those days complaints were made that the show was offensive. My mother unperturbed, made me a ballroom dress, again of crepe paper, and sent me onto the stage clutching my large golliwog. The golly had been acquired by collecting labels off the back of Robertson's marmalade jars. Even at that young age I sensed we had committed a *faux pas*, and judging by the puzzled expression on everyone's faces, it was safe to assume that no one had a clue what I was meant to be.

It's fair to say that cruises hold no allure for me as an adult after my previous experiences, which is not surprising, really.

CHAPTER 6

BOOBITUS

My unfortunate cruising experience leaving Australia left me painfully thin, not that I had an ounce of spare flesh on me prior to my Edam cheese nightmare. When we finally arrived in England in July 1974, I was due to start boarding school that September.

I turned up clutching my favourite soft toy, still resembling a stick insect and subjected to an enforced diet to fatten me up imposed by my mother. It didn't work – I was destined to remain thin. My friends at school jokingly called me a bag of bones and one endearingly nicknamed me Skinnywinnyma. Charming! Luckily I had a sense of humour and settled into boarding school life much as my three sisters before me had.

One of the associated drawbacks of being so thin was the total lack of the acquisition of boobs. Much to my chagrin my three older sisters all had them and sister number three, Caroline, was blessed with more than her fair share. I may not have had boobs but I did have Boobitus.

Boobitus? Ouch! What? My nickname for sore boobs actually. Now come on ladies, there must be hundreds of you out there who know what I am talking about. Yes… plenty of sore boob moments in my life to recount which is ironic really, considering my chest closely resembles an ironing board with two gnat bites.

Developing boobs was my first experience of Boobitus. If ever there was a correlation between developing boob pain and the end result, I should have put Jordan in the shade. Sadly, in my case it was all pain and no gain. Now my sixteen year-old daughter Jocelyn on the other hand (you remember the one who laughs in the face of *Thrush*) has never had sore boobs. And to add insult to injury she is blessed with quite an impressive pair. She certainly does not take after me in that department.

Anyway, once my chest had stopped growing – ha, ha – there was the delight of pre-menstrual boobs to contend with. Wow, they can be painful, but yes you've guessed it Jocelyn doesn't know about that either. Lucky girl. Where did I go wrong?

Pregnancy boobs – aaah yes! Well at least there was the added advantage of seeing my gnat bites grow. Nothing as impressive as my friends whose boobs grew exponentially as pregnancy proceeded but a small bump is better than a gnat bite. I remember peering in wonder the day my milk came in. It was the first time in my life I had a chest resembling the female form – albeit a modest B cup but positively Raquel Welsh for me. However, they hurt for England and breast feeding meant total agony for days.

I did have the last laugh though. I may have been flat-chested but boy could I produce prodigious amounts of milk and left all my mammary enhanced friends in awe of my ability to feed my twin sons with no trouble. My husband James even used to call me his chief milker. True, not very romantic, but at least I remain safe in the knowledge that gravity will never see my boobs down by my waist.

It would be fair to say that over the years the odd moment has crossed my mind to have a boob job, but to be honest the thoughts of silicone bags being entombed in your body, with the associated risk of leaking is not very appealing. So let's just say that I shall stick with my lot now that I am fifty. Who knows, there may even be menopausal Boobitus (if such a thing exists) to look forward to. Watch this space.

CHAPTER 7

BAGS OF SPACE

Space was something of a premium when I moved in 1986 as a single twenty-three year-old, postgraduate, career girl from a rental property in Bedford to live and work in London. Property prices were outstripping the rest of the country at an alarming rate. Gardens were invariably small and an extra couple of feet cost the earth... literally.

By the time I married in November 1993 the housing market had remained strong and even though James and I both had flats to sell we could still only afford a house with a *bijou* garden.

So one of the main reasons for leaving London in January 2001 with James and our three young children – Jocelyn, Piers and Hugo – was to get more space. We were on the cusp of starting a cellar conversion on our Victorian terraced home when James declared the very day we had received final consent to commence the works that he didn't want to live in London anymore and he wanted out of BMW car sales after twenty years. To say I was amazed and the builders flabbergasted would be an understatement. Well you too might have been a little surprised by such events, especially as we had spent five grand on drawings and planning permission. However it was true that we were able to afford a whole lot more house and garden by moving out to the sticks. And so we did. Some friends were envious and others horrified at the prospect of sheep and no coffee shops. These friends would be the very ones who used to love to come and visit for long summer weekends to escape the smoke.

Unfazed by the unknown we put the house on the market. James started a marketing course and life as we knew it changed overnight. We didn't even know where we were going to live – all we had in our heads was an abstract concept of finding more room and a better quality of life for our family. As a temporary measure we planned to live with Grandpa Robert – James' father – who was in his eighties and living alone following the death of his wife some years previously.

Robert lived in a huge house in Berkshire with a wonderful garden and had all the space we craved and more. As he rattled around in just a few rooms the rest was left to the kids to gleefully explore. Much to their delight and my horror the stair gate didn't fit the enormous staircase so they were off in all directions and I was left to chase them. Even more exciting was Robert's stairlift which they loved to ride on, perched precariously on his lap.

Prior to our arrival Robert had managed with the services of his cleaning lady who was also in her eighties and had been with him longer than anyone could remember and certainly before the invention of the hoover! She was so ancient that she clung to the hoover rather like a Zimmer frame, and to say her cleaning abilities were at best limited would be being frugal with the truth. So she was gently pensioned off with a generous settlement and I became responsible for keeping our newly found space clean.

Space had been one of the great luxuries afforded by my father's job in the Foreign Office until he retired in 1985. All the properties allocated to our family over the years to live in abroad were large and sometimes came with staff to clean and garden. As such it inevitably seemed strange as a child to return after a foreign tour (usually lasting a couple of years) to my parents' small semi-detached house in England with its postage stamp garden.

The Northern Territory of Australia, where we lived in the early 70s in particular provided an amazing outdoor life and we would often drive for miles in the Australian outback to enjoy a picnic in solitude. Similarly, in the 60s when my parents were in Kampala, Uganda, my father liked to take us off to look at wild life or just randomly stop for a picnic in the middle of nowhere. On one such occasion we had settled down to eat, when a native Karamojong man at least six foot six inches tall and totally naked appeared, clutching his small handmade wooden stool which the locals carried. A little bit disconcerting you might think for the average person to have some naked stranger breathing down their neck whilst indulging in a picnic. But not for my family! Oh no, my father beckoned him over and he joined us with a few words of Swahili from my mother who had gleaned her vocabulary from Salvanus, our house manservant. He was greatly respected in our home and I was without doubt somewhat fearful of him but one night he was to be my hero.

I was asleep with my sister Caroline who would have been about twelve, to suddenly waken and find the room alive with literally thousands of locusts which had entered via an open window, attracted by an outside light. I recall screaming in fright and Salvanus rushing in even before my mother could get to us. He was absolutely delighted by the sight of so many locusts he deemed to be a delicacy, and he spent ages gathering them all for a feast.

One particular problem for me when living abroad in far flung tropical destinations was getting used to the plethora of creepy crawlies and snakes. The number of snakes which I saw in Australia did nothing to help my snake phobia which still plagues me as an adult. I used to do a lot of horse riding with my parents in Australia where snakes would invariably cross your path but the horses had an uncanny sixth sense when it came to detecting their presence. This was especially useful on the annual fourteen mile trotting race which the local stables held. You definitely didn't want to find yourself face to face with some nasty snake in the middle of the bush so if the horse deviated from the chosen track you knew it was doing you a favour.

My snake paranoia stayed with me even in England where the odd harmless grass snake was no great threat. On return from Oz I would sometimes cycle to a nearby newsagents to buy sweets which involved passing a pub with a large chalk board advertising lunchtime snacks. I would pedal furiously past thinking the sign was referring to snakes!

Years later in my late thirties, when I left London and moved with my family to the Midlands English countryside, we bought a house with an acre plus garden surrounded by fields complete with an old bath which housed the resident grass snake. All that space and the snake had to choose my garden to set up home!

I may not have been enamoured by snakes but I did love Australia, as did my father who was determined to return to the country after his two-and-a-half-year tour ended. We were also obliged to return to the UK, not least because my two eldest sisters were getting married.

By coincidence my great-grandfather had emigrated to Australia and dropped dead at a ripe old age in a Melbourne street. Little more was known other than he had been buried near the famous opera singer Dame Nellie Melba in a cemetery at Lilydale near Coldstream, Melbourne. When we left Australia my parents decided to drive the 3000 kms from Darwin to Sydney to catch the ship home but on the way we did successfully find my grandfather's grave which was unmarked but clearly shown on the cemetery records. When I did my English Language O-Level in 1979 I had to write an essay called *Digging Up The Past* and I wrote all about this experience and how we had spoken to elderly residents who were able to furnish us with the knowledge we were missing.

Australia was not only on the other side of the world, it was so far and prohibitively expensive to fly to, that it might as well have been a different planet. My two eldest sisters had left home to pursue degrees and professions by the time my parents were sent there in 1972. Only my sister Caroline who was still at school was able to fly out courtesy of the Foreign Office. Communication with friends and family left at home was limited to the odd phone call and mostly letters. With the advent of new technology the world is now a much smaller place and so very different to the one I knew as a child.

CHAPTER 8

CALL ME

Don't you think one of the wonderful things about modern technology is the simplicity of communication? Debbie may live thousands of miles away in New Zealand but with the availability of Skype it's possible to see each other and chat whenever we like. My parents who are both in their eighties determinedly refuse to embrace any such thing and remain resolutely entrenched in some dinosaur world. Computers are alien to them. Even their mobile phone is the size of a brick and no doubt manufactured when dinosaurs ruled the earth. They may own a mobile but frankly it is quite pointless, because they never charge it and use it so infrequently that they actually forget how to use it. Unbelievable but true.

On one occasion about seven years ago they came to visit me and my family on a coach from Yorkshire, where they had lived since 1985. My father had long decided that motorway driving was too stressful but in truth he was doing the other drivers on the road a great service by not subjecting them to his driving prowess. I certainly have avoided getting in his car for many a year and have come up with every excuse I could muster.

On the day, I had agreed to meet them at the Northampton coach station at a predetermined time with a firm assurance they would let me know if there was a delay. This necessitated resurrecting their mobile from its enforced retirement, and what an event that was! My father insisted on testing the mobile and tried to phone me. Now most normal human beings would probably just dial the number and say hello but oh no, not my father! I was greeted by "Hello, hello. Testing, testing. One, two, three; Garnett speaking." A little odd, I know but for many years it had been one of his strange idiosyncrasies to answer the home telephone with "Garnett speaking" in his dulcet Yorkshire tones.

Anyway, I arrived at the appointed time and waited and waited and waited. Finally I tried calling them. However, their mobile was switched off. After forty-five minutes and endless fruitless attempts to get hold of them I was steaming. Doesn't it just drive you crazy, that sort of thing? My three children were fed up sat in the car, and to cap it all there was nowhere to park, so I ended up driving around the coach pick up area in a loop, like a rat on a wheel. When they did finally arrive I demanded to know through gritted welcoming teeth why they hadn't called me and why the mobile was switched off. Apparently it was to save the battery and as their bag had been placed in the overhead locker (with the phone in) it was inconvenient to reach for it. Infuriating. Let's just say phones are not their strong point.

For years my parents managed to survive without a phone in the house. Any important calls meant plodding off down the road to the nearest red BT box. These invariably smelled of wee and were often out of order. Why anyone should choose to use the telephone box as a convenience I have no idea. And if it was in working order, you could guarantee there would be someone monopolising it without the slightest intention of stopping yacking until they had spoken to everyone they knew including the dog! A friend of mine told me she had had the audacity to knock on the glass once when some woman had talked for three weeks without stopping for breath. The woman appeared menacingly at the door declaring that my friend had nice teeth and wondered if she would like to keep them. Charming, I'm sure. And as you also needed a wheel barrow's worth of correct change to make a call – which was irritatingly periodically interrupted by 'beep, beep, beep', as the money ran out, it could be a frustrating experience.

So very occasionally for convenience and retention of sanity we would call in to our neighbour, who happened to be my godmother and use her phone, always leaving a shilling or two on the side. I suppose you could say that at least people only phoned if they had something important to say. Unlike today – how much inane nonsense is sent via text, e-mail and Facebook? I expect the art of conversation will probably be redundant soon as we resort to these other forms of communication and grunting will become acceptable speech.

It wasn't until 1974 when my parents returned to England from Australia that we acquired a house phone. And *that* was only because the American couple who had rented their house in their absence had fitted one. The newly acquired phone was sited in the hallway, which was freezing cold in winter, no doubt to dissuade anyone from making a call lasting longer than ten seconds. And it was impossible to hold a private conversation with a boyfriend as my mother would always ensure she had a reason to be in the hall just as the phone rang. I am sure that this phone phobia is the reason why in later years as an adult I ensured I had loads of phones all over the house, as well as mobiles. And I hate phones in hallways! When my parents moved to Yorkshire on retirement they had the obligatory hall phone. After years of calling them, my mother would always have to go and get her kitchen stool to sit on to talk. Why they didn't just get a phone fitted in the sitting room I have no idea but old habits die hard. In the end I bought them a portable phone so they could chat from anywhere in the house. Even this technology was met with suspicion but the real trouble started when I suggested an answering machine. My father was convinced that if they did not answer, it would be obvious to any self respecting burglar that they were out and they would be robbed. I attempted to point out that it *was* possible to be in but not choose to answer, as it may be inconvenient – you might be in the bath or eating or chatting to the neighbours' cat. They were not to be convinced and the answering machine was invariably not switched on. That would have been fine but they would then complain that they hadn't heard from me in a long while. The fact that I had attempted to phone and leave a message but had been unable to do so fell on deaf ironic ears.

Of course today's kids know nothing of these challenges as they are all armed with the latest technology. My children just can't understand how I can possibly survive with my basic mobile. The fact that it makes and receives calls and sends texts and takes photos is apparently so old hat. But I don't need it to wash up on a Wednesday, or bake a cake on a Thursday and I refuse to indulge in Facebook or tweet so it really is fine for my needs and I certainly don't weep into my pillow at night because I am not the proud owner of a Blackberry.

CHAPTER 9

LOCKED OUT

There have been moments in my life when I would have been glad of any type of mobile – flash or otherwise – to get me out of a sticky situation. It would be fair to say I have in the past had a strange knack for getting locked out of houses. Back in the early 1990s, in my pre-children, pre-mobile ownership days, I lived with James in a Victorian mid-terraced house in South West London. James was an avid cricket fan, a sport which I detested, so on a Sunday he would disappear to play cricket and I would sometimes go off horse riding in Richmond Park.

On one particular day which was sunny, I had returned all hot and sweaty to my house, desperate to rid myself of my clinging jodhpurs and long boots. I stripped off in the kitchen down to my G-string pants and T-shirt and opened the kitchen door for some air. As the weather was so good I intended to do some gardening but first decided to empty the rubbish bin. We didn't have any front garden as such, just a small bit in front of the bay window screened by a high, immaculately kept, privet hedge. My pride and joy. The bin was tucked away out of sight behind the hedge so I quickly nipped out the front door to dump the rubbish bag. It was not my day however, as a gust of wind from the open back door slammed the front door and I was left stranded in my knickers. You will appreciate that sinking OMG moment. For a fleeting second I panicked but convinced myself one of my neighbours would be in and if all else failed I could climb over the shared back fence and get in to the house again. Fine, except they weren't in. So there I was, stuck, half-undressed, hiding behind my hedge with James not due for a least another six hours and no phone. I had an old mate from university who lived a few minutes' walk away but it was a respectable area and I could hardly have sauntered through the streets half-naked and acted as if all was well with the world.

So I found myself mentally assessing all the people who lived in our road for suitability to save me. It wasn't a very long road and I certainly recognised most of the residents and knew a few but this was London and people generally kept themselves to themselves. The thoughts of charging up to a complete stranger in my G-string and saying, "I know you don't know me but could you let me sit in your house for six hours until my husband returns" seemed somewhat ludicrous. However, needs must, so when after an hour I spied a potential saviour – a woman who lived several doors away – I abandoned caution to the wind. I tried to minimise my public exposure by charging up to her as fast as I could, trying to catch her before she disappeared. To say she was a little surprised to have some semi-naked, deranged woman appear on her doorstep would be an understatement! Fortunately for me she saw the funny side and let me borrow a pair of leggings so I was at least able to walk to my friend's house (albeit barefoot) who thought the whole thing was hilarious.

Quite a few years later following my family's eight month sojourn with Grandpa Robert, we ended up in a small village in Northamptonshire. We gleefully exchanged the proceeds of our London terraced house complete with postage stamp garden for a large cottage with over an acre of land and rural views. This time there were no neighbours as such. Whilst we were deemed to be in the village we were set well back down a long gravelled drive and surrounded by fields grazed by noisy sheep.

One day whilst the kids were at school I had been engrossed in dull paperwork and decided to have a break and go and clean out the hen house. I exited the boot-room as I had hundreds of times before complete with regulation wellies and pulled the door behind me. The second I closed the door I froze – I had locked myself out and did not have a hidden spare key or a mobile on me. *Déjà vu* moment or what? As I had the school run in a couple of hours' time it became imperative to break-in and get the car keys. Easier said than done. The cottage had been fastidiously fitted with window locks, so to avoid smashing any glass I set my sights on the cellar which had part louvered windows. I figured I could probably get in that way if I persevered, which I did. I painstakingly removed all the glass panels – with some difficulty as I had deliberately glued them in place to deter any would-be burglars – how ironic. Finally after a lot of effort and not a shortage of bad language – luckily only witnessed by a few intrigued sheep in the field – I managed to lower myself and jump into the cellar. That was all very well but now I was technically locked in the cellar. I could not climb up and access the way I had come in and the flight of stone stairs up to the hallway were met with a solid oak latch door. If ever a Houdini was needed, this was it. The latch was on the hall side so I rummaged for a screwdriver in the tool box and tried to lift the latch which was very stiff and as I was unsighted in the gloom, no easy feat. I was becoming seriously miffed when finally, hey presto the latch lifted and I could claim the accolade of having broken into my own house.

Feeling rather smug I shot off down the other end of the cottage to unlock the boot-room door. To my absolute incredulity the door wasn't locked. In fact it couldn't be, unless you had a key. Well, I laughed until I cried. The whole thing was just so stupid, but I dined out on that tale for a while.

CHAPTER 10

PETS GALORE

I actually had a canary called Tale when I was ten and living in Australia. Apart from the odd dull gold fish, won at the local fair, I had never had a pet before. My father and I were both allergic to cats and dogs so that was a no goer. I was even very allergic to horses but persevered as I loved to ride. Both my parents and I had learned to ride in Australia at a very bohemian stables run by an ancient Irish woman, Mrs Flockhart. Her bizarre home was so open-plan that it allowed all the animals to wander in and out at leisure and it was no surprise to find hens in her sitting room. My mother had a particular fondness for a white mare called Breeze and never was there a more apt name. This equine would fart for England and was positively jet propelled!

When we moved away from London to embrace countryside life we decided to have hens, thinking it would be good for the kids to have some pets – albeit not indoor ones. I knew nothing about hens but we bravely went to a local farmer to see if he had any to sell. He did and generously threw in a cockerel as well for free. Little did I know this cockerel would be such a control freak. No wonder the farmer wanted rid. He was a nasty piece of work and quite aggressive even towards me, the hand that fed him. The children insisted on naming all five hens and the cockerel although I was not so sure this was a good idea. Names suggest attachment and Mr Fox was never too far away. Anyway the cockerel was called Paxo, an irony which passed the children by.

Of course the trouble with hens and cockerels is the excessive pillaging that goes on. My children would enquire with earnest faces why Paxo was being so mean to the hens and jumping on their backs. Well, what would you have said? And the end result of all this meanness... yes, broody hens. I had no idea that hens could be broody and not even have any eggs to sit on. Some would sit in a stupefied trance for days on end on nothing more than a pile of straw. Others would sit on a clutch of eggs with enthusiastic vigour, only to find after twenty-one days the eggs had not been fertilised, so it had all been a waste of time. And believe me, hens can look depressed – *I* should know! All this egg sitting meant no egg laying, so if all the hens went broody it was a pain. To be fair, it was exciting if a sitting session led to real fluffy chicks, which it sometimes did. I then turned into some kind of hen-midwife resuscitating the chicks by putting them up my T-shirt onto a warm tummy and then into an oven mitt on top of the Aga. All a far cry from my London, Kings Road shopping days. The trouble with baby chicks, cute as they may be, is that some will become future cockerels. You really, really don't want more than one cockerel. No wonder the farmer was happy to fob one off on us. They fight and argue all day long. Plus you have the dawn chorus, which believe me, is bad enough with one. When finally my patience had been challenged too far, I resolved to be cockerel free and life was far more peaceful after that.

One of the main drawbacks I discovered whilst keeping hens was their food, which left in the run attracted a lot of squirrels, birds and rats. An expensive business. And not just any old rats but rats the size of articulated lorries. Believe me, you want to give them a wide berth. Such is country life.

As for bedtime, our feathered friends really could be little buggers. On most days as dusk settled they would put themselves to bed and tuck up safely in the hen house for the night. But if the odd one left it a bit late they couldn't work out their way back to the run. I can only assume their eyesight was poor or they just took great pleasure in winding me up. So it was left to me, the chief mother hen to go hunting in the dark with a torch and round them up in all weathers. Then they would have the cheek to look slightly paralysed with fear when I grabbed them and wedged them under my armpit with a severe ticking off. Better me than the fox.

If I thought my hens were challenging, my neighbour's peacocks were in a league of their own. At one point I think we counted twenty of them and they much preferred our garden to their own to wreck and deposit their nasty tar like poo which stuck to surfaces like super glue. Whilst they were very beautiful they were incredibly destructive and would nip the heads off all our gorgeous flowers. As I was an avid gardener they were about as popular as meat is to a vegetarian. I confess they drove me scatty with their horrendous screeching. I often lost the plot first thing in the morning when I could see them all gathered for another assault on my garden. To the kids' huge amusement

I could often be seen rushing out in a super rage, usually naked apart from a hastily put on pair of wellies, to chase them like some totally crazed woman and yell abuse to no avail. And to think I used to be normal before I embraced country life!

Children being children, they were not satisfied with hens or peacocks and wanted something else – namely rabbits. Did I have mug written on my face? I must have, because I relented with promises from my kids that *they* would feed and look after them. Ha, fat chance! I became chief and then sole carer of two cute bunnies but I was so allergic to them I thought they would do me in. Happily I eventually acquired an immunity to them – just as well, really. But then we had the new arrivals after some serious rabbit bonking. They never stopped! Eight... yes, *eight*, super cute, baby bunnies appeared. How gorgeous they were hopping about the kitchen with us all totally entranced. Not so funny when they escaped from their run and I had to charge around the garden like some madwoman scooping them up. Off to the pet shop it was with them all and I made an executive decision to have two boy rabbits. Well how was I to know they would embrace homosexuality with gay abandon? You have no idea!

That was a sufficient foray into the pet world until I moved to a house which came with a large pond, complete with twenty koi – large ones at that. Much like the hens I did not have a clue but naively believed the previous owners when they said they were no trouble at all. The pond man apparently came just a few times a year at little cost and all was well. I lived to rue the day I fell for *that* one. After the first two £400 bills I nearly passed out. This was all to do with balancing the eco-friendly bacteria of the pond. I don't mind admitting that I didn't feel particularly friendly towards the fish, bacteria or the pond man at that point. My neighbour often used to say she had seen a heron flying over and wondered whether the koi would be OK. I used to go to bed at night and pray for the heron to come and not be on a diet. Said heron regrettably never materialised, although he may have been challenged by the menu, as most of the koi were sumo-sized and more likely to eat the heron.

I had done my best to clean the filters and scoop endless leaves off the pond but to no avail. The pond never had that crystal clear look which I coveted – pond man or no pond man. Anyway as my bank balance depleted and the pond man seemed to get ever richer on the proceeds of my ignorance, I decided to redress the balance. Surely it couldn't be rocket science to maintain a pond? So I threw caution to the wind and dispensed with his services. Second I disregarded all concerns for a balanced pond ecosystem with all the associated turgid detail about good and bad bacteria that I had been subjected to. I appreciate that it's good to be passionate about your work but I had glazed over on more than one occasion when the pond man tried to wow me with the science of pond maintenance. Watching paint dry would have been a lesser torture. I figured getting rid of him was a bit like turning your back on organic foods when your finances can no longer justify the alleged benefits relative to cost. In the end you don't notice the difference. So I committed the cardinal sin of hosing down all the filters with clean tap water instead of agitating them in the pond water. It seemed to me that all you were doing was putting all the crap back in the pond again, all to avoid not upsetting the good bacteria. Would you believe it, the pond has never looked better and the koi certainly look happy. They are quite a satisfying pet – beautiful to watch and quite tame, eating out of your hand and allowing themselves to be stroked. Much like Pavlov's dogs, who salivated when a bell was rung, I only have to open the shed door where their food is kept and they sprint over like Olympic swimmers to be fed and show their appreciation.

You might think that twenty large fish would be enough for one family but we are devils for punishment. About a year ago I visited a very large garden centre which had an amazing aquatic centre. The fish were gorgeous and compelling to watch and before I knew it a desire for tropical fish was on the wish list. But first I needed to locate a suitable piece of furniture to sit the tank on having dismissed all the shop options. After some hunting the perfect piece of distressed furniture came up on eBay. The bid was submitted and won and I was to collect it the next day after a planned drinks party.

Fine, except the following day I had the hangover from hell and could hardly stand, let alone contemplate the collection of furniture. The very prospect of lifting my head off the pillow was questionable. You may know that feeling when you are sure that death may be preferable to the one hundred monkeys banging drums in your head. However, the furniture was eventually collected and the fish bought and settled in over the next few weeks. I had deliberately chosen a selection of community fish all content to live harmoniously together. The trouble is they are a bit *too* friendly. Remember those rabbits,

well they pale into insignificance when it comes to matters of fish ardour. What a rampant lot they are, always chasing each other and sneaking off to hide in the ship wreck. Up to no good as we know, judging by the profusion of babies they produce on a weekly basis. Never mind 'at it like rabbits'. More like 'at it like fish!'

CHAPTER 11

BUN IN THE OVEN

All this talk of reproduction reminds me of my own experience. Whilst I have produced three children, albeit twins on one occasion – two for the price of one in true Tesco style – I had a great deal of trouble making babies. Perhaps I should have visited my local pet shop and asked for sound advice from the resident rabbits and fish. Or I could have referred to an old school friend who openly admitted she and her husband never had sex unless of course they wanted another child. All she had to do was look at him and she was banged up good and proper, so to speak. As for me, getting pregnant was definitely difficult, keeping the pregnancy viable even more difficult and as for labour… Well, let's just say it was very memorable. I didn't have to resort to IVF but did suffer a number of miscarriages before I finally became pregnant with Jocelyn. Delighted though I was to be pregnant, I could not have conceived (no pun intended) how ill this so called normal state could make you feel. Morning sickness… What a joke! How about all-day sickness, just for a laugh? The dreadful sensitivity to smells like the mix of perfume and aftershave on the London Underground and the sudden strange disliking for foods and drinks that had previously been a pleasure were all to be embraced. It would be no exaggeration to claim I spent an inordinate amount of my day being acquainted with the loo. When I was about eight weeks pregnant I went to Rome for a five day break. All the ancient artefacts and sites were totally fascinating but devoid of the one crucial facility. No surprise really.

When the big day finally arrived I had resolved I would be OK as I had a high pain threshold, having suffered from a bad back off and on for a number of years. My antenatal classes with the NCT (National Childbirth Trust) had been enlightening and amusing if totally dishonest about the level of pain to be experienced. Of course pain is subjective. My mother had apparently given birth in excruciating silence. If it hurts that much how can you not screech? I did meet some great people on the NCT classes and one lovely couple went on to be wonderful friends. Sixteen years later we are still firm friends and share reciprocal godparent duties. The classes were held weekly in different parent to be houses on a rota basis. The men used to be shepherded into the kitchen to discuss I know not what, whilst the birds were incarcerated in the sitting room sprawled on the floor practising pretend contractions. How you can pretend to have a contraction I have no idea but we all participated with enthusiasm anyway.

The big day started innocuously enough – slight contractions, moving inexorably onto more determined 'ouch' contractions. I dutifully went off to St Thomas' Hospital in London to be assessed for progress and was more than a bit dismayed to find I had a long way to go, so went home for a hot bath. By the time we returned I was climbing the car walls. As James drew up at traffic lights we found ourselves next to a police car. Another big contraction swept over me and I let rip.

I remember James asking me not to yell quite so loudly in case the officers in the car thought I was being abducted. I'm not sure what they thought but they didn't do anything and we continued on our journey. We arrived and I struggled into the lift bent triple much to the alarm of the other people sharing the lift with us. But this was only the start. Twenty hours of sheer torture later with no gas – it had run out – and a student male nurse by my side getting experience (poor him), I finally gave birth. My final screeches were met by a female doctor who told me to shut up and if I had had the strength I swear I would have knocked her out. I said afterwards I didn't know it was possible to hurt so much and not be dead.

Now you might think that this would put you off having babies for ever but twenty-one months later, having suffered an ectopic pregnancy in the interim, I was expecting twins. I didn't quite know how to react when I found out at only six weeks gestation I was carrying twins. Whilst they ran in the family, having identical twin uncles, this was not a scenario I had considered. I think I was just amazed and grateful to be pregnant again. This time I had all the associated pregnancy traits to be juggled with a toddler which definitely meant extra *knackerdom*. I'm not sure humans are really cut out to carry more than one baby even if rabbits do so with consummate ease.

The area of London I lived in at the time was known as Nappy Valley due to the prolific thirty-something, ex-professional, IVF-assisted women who gave birth. Twins and triplets were a common sight, so I blended in with no trouble. Despite starting the pregnancy at a scrap of just over eight stone, I put on more than three stone during the term and was totally huge. So huge I struggled to move and breathe at the end. By thirty-seven weeks I begged my consultant to let me be induced as I could stand no more. He had enthusiastically embraced the whole process, encouraging me to eat two chocolate bars a day to keep my strength up. My local friends had taken this to heart and would regularly deliver chocolate bars to my doorstep until I had a hidden supply of chocolate I could not bear to eat. Can you imagine? The end result was I felt like some fatted seal.

Thank heavens my consultant took pity on me and I was induced but my two boys had no intention of doing the honourable thing. I remained in labour for about seven hours and then all hell let loose. Apparently the heartbeat of one of the twins could not be regulated satisfactorily and an emergency caesarean was foisted on me. That would have been fine – scary though it was – but worryingly James appeared in a white gown and what looked like wellies to assist. Would that have instilled great confidence in *you*? On the way into the operating theatre, I kid you not: two of the medical staff pushing my trolley had a major row. I offered to hold the drip, which caused more argument. What can you do?

It all worked out perfectly in the end. Piers and Hugo were born and a super respectable seven pounds three ounces and six pounds fifteen ounces. Apart from chronic wind after the operation I felt bloody fantastic, losing what felt like three whales in weight from my waist. And… Wait for it… Not a stretch mark in sight. OMG. Within ten days, I was back in normal clothes, which drove my post-pregnancy friends into a frenzy of incredulity.

CHAPTER 12

DRIVEN CRAZY

Speaking of incredulity, new acquaintances when I moved to Northamptonshire were equally incredulous that I had never learned to drive. Believe it or not I was nearly thirty-eight before I finally succumbed to the inevitable need to obtain my license. When I just had Jocelyn it was easy to hop on a bus or tube in London and get about. When you have a double pram with twins and a two year-old hanging on to your left leg, you are looking at a whole different ball game. I'm not quite sure why I was so phobic about the whole driving experience. However, the move to the countryside and my daughter starting school in a village four miles from our home made it an urgent necessity to get behind the wheel, especially as there was no bus service in our village. Mind you, I say there was no bus service but that was not strictly speaking true. Bizarrely, the village green notice board provided details of buses you could allegedly catch but the odd thing was they never returned!

So I managed to find a very patient and tolerant man to teach me to drive which is just as well really, as I used to bring the kids with me on my lessons (much to his amazement) – all strapped into baby seats and bribed into silence with a packet of crisps. Anyway I passed my test with huge relief and my life was never the same again.

The day after my test I was excited at the prospect of driving on my own. Or at least as on your own as you can be with children in tow. So I enthusiastically set off with the boys to Milton Keynes which was a good forty-five minute drive away. I arrived without getting lost much to my surprise (having an appalling sense of direction) and tried to park. However, it would have been easier to have arranged for tea with the Queen than find a parking space. I drove around for half an hour hunting the elusive space and eventually had to concede defeat and drive home. As if that wasn't bad enough I missed my turning for the dual carriageway and ended up on the motorway, which was an alarming 'OMG, didn't mean to do that' new driver moment.

At the time I drove a second-hand Golf and James had a two-seater sports car which was definitely not child-friendly, and was his pride and joy.

One day he was in the garage rubbing down some furniture with sandpaper and our son Hugo who was nearly two was with him. Unfortunately Hugo decided to help his dad by sandpapering his car. To say James was furious would be an understatement. In fact he lost the art of speech and looked much like a goldfish opening and closing his mouth when he tried to tell me what had happened. For a split second I thought he was on the verge of a heart attack. Pets and kids, eh?

This was not the first time the children had caused heart stopping moments. Whilst living with Grandpa Robert we had a night to remember. Piers and Hugo had been put to bed and I had planned to settle down later that evening to watch a Bond film with James. I had popped upstairs to check on the twins a few times because although they were not even two, their climbing skills would have put the average orangutan to shame. They would climb out of their cots and do gym-like circuits until they eventually flopped asleep, usually in some obscure position. Just before the film started I nipped upstairs expecting to see them 'zedding' away, but they were nowhere to be seen. I knew they couldn't have got out of the room as the door handle was too high and stiff. There was only one place they could be. I wrenched back the curtain and found them out for the count on the deep windowsill. But there was blood everywhere and my heart certainly hopped a few beats. Thankfully it was not nearly as bad as it looked. They had knocked a picture off the wall and the glass had shattered onto the sill and little fingers had been cut. Ironically, I happened to be wearing a twenty-four hour heart monitor trace following an irregular heartbeat diagnosis. This was definitely one of those heart stopping moments and it certainly made for interesting reading when my consultant checked my results. Luckily all three of us were fine and none the worse for wear.

Fast-forward a few years and the boys, aged seven, were loving the freedom of countryside life. They had become very friendly with the peacock neighbour's son Freddy, who was a couple of years older than them. Village life generally meant kids of all ages mixed although not always in a positive way. I was a little flummoxed when one day the boys came home full of chat with Freddy about an older girl's vibrator. Try explaining *that one* to a seven-year-old! That aside, he was a pleasant little boy and always polite, so a big tick in the you can come and play again box.

During the summer holidays endless hours were spent playing in the garden and fields getting deliciously grubby. I had no issue with dirt – after all boys will be boys – as long as it migrated no further than the boot-room. I would stand like some vulture at the door waiting for any filthy urchins to appear and they would all be divested of clothes at an alarming speed, much to Freddy's amazement. He saw the funny side however, and didn't mind wearing some ridiculously small clothes belonging to Piers and Hugo whilst I did a quick wash and returned him home later reasonably clean and fluffy. I don't know if his mother marvelled at his ability to return home cleaner than he had left. She probably thought all the dirt had washed off in the lakes which were on their farm land.

Those lakes were like a magnet for the boys who didn't seem at all fussed by the water rats or the grass snakes which freaked me out. The lakes to them just meant fun, albeit dangerous fun and it was virtually impossible to keep them away. One day the boys had gone off to play with strict instructions to pop back occasionally and not go near the lakes. Who was I kidding? Rather too many hours passed without hide nor hair of them being seen so I started to worry. I am not one of those over-protective, wrap your kids up in cotton wool variety but having yelled like a fishwife across the fields with zero response (apart from some disgruntled sheep baaing at me to shut up) I went on a quick sortie of the village. Still no luck. Two hours later and I was becoming frantic in a controlled suppressed sort of way – never a good thing. I could hear shooting down by the far fields where the practise range was and it crossed my mind that that was where they might have gone. I headed off with a purposeful I'm going to ring your necks stride when I spotted the three of them. The stalker and the stalked faced each other. The boys clinging to Freddy looked a lot like rabbits caught in the glare of car headlights, totally paralysed with terror. Mind you I think I might have been afraid of myself too. They frantically scuttled about like spiders trying to hide behind a hedge even though they knew they had been spotted. When I screamed "Come here!" it lacked any control or suppression of anger and Freddy bolted for his life. My boys thought better of running away and also prudently avoided speaking to me whilst I ranted and chastised them on the walk back. I was so relieved to see them and have them home and safe but was also furious as you might imagine. As for Freddy, he lived to tell the tale and kept a low profile for a few weeks until I had calmed down. Smart boy!

CHAPTER 13

ON THE MOVE

I believe that I was considered to be reasonably smart as a teenager by my parents, although having attended a private school there were a lot of pretty bright cookies in the biscuit barrel. However, I held my own as best I could and achieved nine O-Levels and three A-Levels with a determination to prove I was no dumb blonde. Mind you dumb blondes usually have 'Page three' chests and, as I had no chest at all, this left me in a class of my own. And unfortunately unless you were in the top set for everything I'm sure my school had you marked down as some dimwit.

As my parents were often abroad with my father's job it fell to my eldest sister Gill as my appointed guardian (who happened to be a French teacher) to attend parents' evenings. On one such occasion my English teacher had the misfortune to suggest that as I was quite pretty I would probably make a good secretary. I must admit I was quite surprised to see her alive and kicking the next day after Gill had virtually torn every limb from her body – metaphorically speaking of course.

All these qualifications were all very well but I didn't really have a clue what I wanted to be. Did you when you were growing up? I mean does anyone really wake up one day and say I'm going to be a rocket scientist and then really truly become one? I never aspired to be a hairdresser which so many teenage girls seem to want to become for some inexplicable reason. Perhaps they think you get to play with hair all day long. I suspect it's more likely you end up listening to a load of clients offloading their woes on you whilst you endlessly sweep up hair and stand for so many hours that varicose veins come knocking on your door. Besides which, I was academically career driven with successful older sisters to emulate and university beckoned. However, still being unsure what career I wanted to pursue I elected to take an American Studies degree which covered a broad range of subjects, namely American law, literature, history, politics, thought and culture. In fact, everything you did and didn't want to know about America. My mother had American citizenship courtesy of her father and Debbie had by then lived in the USA for seven years so there was a family interest in the country. My parents had even toyed with the idea of retiring there.

I may not have known what career path to follow but my father had some strange notion that all four of his daughters would want to be just like him and embark on a career with the Foreign Office. No thanks very much! Yes there were a number of exotic desirable postings to sunny climes and there were also some rather less delightful places one could end up in, especially if you were a single woman.

In the early 80s we ended up in Helsinki, Finland and apart from the impossible language the weather was cold enough to persuade penguins to emigrate. My mother, keen as ever, had bought a Teach Yourself Finnish phrase book. And very usefully (not) the very first phrase was 'He is a priest.' Now I don't know about you but when you are lost or hungry in a foreign country I'm not sure how handy that is. The local residents would probably think you were some kind of nutter rambling on about priests. My mother certainly caused some major confusion the day the removal men arrived to unpack our possessions. At the end of the task she stood there waving her arms saying, "Finish, finish?" A distinct look of puzzlement crossed their brows and it was clear they thought the English woman was unhinged. Just as well she didn't try out her phrase book on them.

And when we had our home contents unpacked in Darwin, Australia, I was mortified when endless rolls of loo paper appeared. I kid you not my mother had heard that loo paper was expensive in Australia and she had calculated how many rolls she thought we would get through during a two-and-a-half year-tour and had them shipped out. One hundred and eight to be precise. Once all the rolls were unpacked one of the removal men turned to my mother and said "That's a hell of a lot of shit paper you've got there, Sheila!" You couldn't make it up!

Over the years I have certainly moved house a great deal. That was the accepted way of life for a diplomat's daughter. By the time I was eighteen, I had lived in Singapore, Yugoslavia, Uganda, Australia, Swaziland and Finland and visited many other countries. I had also already briefly visited New Zealand on one of my cruise experiences with my parents. After leaving home I went on to further travel and accommodated house moves as casually as a hermit crab changes its shell.

After A-Levels I took a year off and spent some months working for my third sister Caroline and her husband Norman, in Javea, Spain where they owned a bar/restaurant called La Panterra Naranja. The Orange Panther. The neon bar sign image which flashed at the prolific abundance of ex-pats bore an uncanny resemblance to the Pink Panther who may well have had something to say about copyright. However this was Spain in the early 80s and nobody seemed to notice or care.

On arrival, having been collected somewhat alarmingly by a drunk Norman I was taken to their home. To say that the accommodation arrangements were a little bohemian would be an understatement. They rented an apartment but despite having lived there for a year when I arrived they had somehow forgotten to unpack. Suitcases were strewn in haphazard fashion in the spare rooms and there was no drinking water or food in the fridge. I concluded with the best humour I could muster that it was purely a place to lay your head and hope not to die of dehydration or starvation. My sister seemed to suffer no ill effects from lack of food, although to be fair she probably survived due to her unique diet which consisted of the local brandy which all the ex-pats imbibed with alarming vigour. The only other occupant was their rather nasty under-fed Alsatian dog called Bimbo, named after the local bread. It would be true to say that despite my lack of flesh I often wondered if Bimbo saw me as a tasty snack as he had a heart-stopping habit of salivating in my presence with a terrifying guttural growl. Fortunately I never was eaten but the whole experience put me off dogs for years.

After Spain it was off to Nottingham University where I shared a flat with seven other girls. All was well until I nearly burned the place down. The fire happened during my first year exams and I had popped a pie in the oven for lunch and gone to my room to revise. The next thing the fire brigade were hauling me out through smoke-filled hallways and I was deposited on the grass next to my semi-cooked pie with a withering "Is this yours?" Unfortunately the chip pan ring had been turned off at the mains and not by the dial so when I put the oven on… Say no more. Fortunately I managed not to cause any mayhem at my next student house – except for the budgie I owned, which had a super-decibelled tweet. One screech was enough to turn my normal Mr Jekyll housemates into Mr Hydes faster than you could blink.

After leaving university I rented part of a shared house in Bedford whilst embarking on a banking career. That was fine except one couple were overtly fond of bonking in the bathroom which happened to be next to my bedroom. Apart from my obvious delight at being subjected to their ardour on a nightly basis, the bathroom much resembled the aftermath of a tsunami following their frolics, so it was with some relief that I moved to Finsbury Park in London.

This time it was a large Victorian four storey house. The owners, a Nigerian couple, lived on the ground floor with their son and the other floors were rented out. I lived on the top floor with an ex-university friend and a girl we found via a property rental agency. The landlord I shall describe as an interesting character. How else do you describe a man who used to beat the hell out of your bedroom door each Saturday morning with no respect for your hangover, demanding his weekly rent wearing a pair of pyjamas with his assets virtually hanging out! He was however amenable enough in his own inimitable way and would sometimes ask we girls to join his family for a glass of wine. It was always best to be otherwise occupied on these occasions as the wine if indeed it was (doubtful) tasted so bad I would try to tip in it their plant pot when they weren't looking. To be offered a second glass was torture personified, and to say you really couldn't possibly have one more when he knew you drank like a fish didn't wash. If you could escape the wine you were doing well. If you escaped being left in the dark, even better. The electricity meters which gobbled fifty pence coins faster than I could earn them were infuriatingly located in the cellar and you guessed it, the cellar was locked and only the landlord had a key, so if he was out bad luck. To add insult to injury I returned from a foreign holiday on one occasion to find not only the pitch dark but my friend's boyfriend in *my* bed as they had had a row. Bloody cheek! This was to mark the end of rental life.

CHAPTER 14

ROMANCE PERSONIFIED

In 1987 the interest rates were sky high for would-be home owners. Conveniently I worked for a bank so was able to get a mortgage at a much less eye watering rate. Those were the days when during the course of a meal with friends, inevitably discussing house prices and how much your house was worth, it had doubled in value by the time the cheese course was served.

I had bravely entered the property market with an ex-boyfriend in August that year. He was very DIY orientated and I learned to tile and even fit sash windows under his critical eye. It was fun doing up our home and after a short fifteen months we sold making a cool £21,000 profit. We left our two bed terraced house in Wood Green, London and moved to a three bedroom house in Turnpike Lane and initially were very happy. We had a lovely home and my career with the bank was going well. My boyfriend's move to France for a six month contract as a structural engineer however was not a success. My relationship foundered after five years together and I moved again from North London to south of the river and bought myself a property close to the trendy wine bars and shops off The Northcote Road in Clapham/Battersea.

Here I was free to explore my DIY and property development skills to my heart's content. Most went according to plan but the discovery of woodworm after I had pulled up and discarded all the hideous carpets was a bit of a pain. So much for the structural survey. It certainly wasn't the most thrilling of things to spend your money on. However needs must and I had the woodworm people sort the problem by pouring endless buckets of foul-smelling solution all over the floorboards. That night there was only one safe place to go unless I wanted to die of asphyxiation, so I locked myself in the bathroom and tucked up in the bath for the night. You would be right in thinking it wasn't the best night's sleep I have ever had. Still, I was only in my late twenties and physically resilient as well as fairly creative and quirkily innovative. My ex had chosen to buy me out of all our household possessions so I had the rather time consuming job of hunting for new furniture. As my parents were due to visit and I hadn't got around to finding a suitable kitchen table I decided to utilise the ironing board and even laid it with a tablecloth for that special Savoy dining experience. Well you can't say I didn't try.

About eight months after moving, in May 1992, I met my future husband in a wine bar on the other side of London. Coincidentally James lived only a couple of roads away from my place. The first time I was invited over after a night out on the tiles drinking more than our fair share of red wine, we walked into kitchen disaster. The flat above was being completely gutted and all the upheaval had caused the old Victorian ceiling plaster to collapse. Whilst it wasn't the most romantic of evenings clearing up all the mess, at least we hadn't been standing there when it happened. It would have given a whole new meaning to the expression being plastered.

Years later I had another near first date disaster. I had separated from James after seventeen years of marriage and found myself back on the dating scene again at the age of forty-seven. This left me in a bit of a quandary as to how to meet someone new. All my friends were either married or in long term relationships. I could have gone to pubs and wine bars to meet new people but it's tricky as a single woman if you don't want to give the wrong impression. Believe me once you are single, other women see you as some kind of potential husband thief and cling to their spouses like barnacles to a shipwreck.

I eventually decided the best course of action was to join a dating website. By the time I had completed the very long online questionnaire, which seemed to even want to know what colour knickers I wore, I doubted how any would-be suitor could possibly not know as much about me as I knew about myself. However it did sort the wheat from the chaff so to speak and provided me with suitable profiles to peruse. However words can be deceiving. It's a strange thing trying to decide if you are attracted to someone without a photo. You would be amazed how many blokes omitted to post a picture but as I ventured into the Match Affinity world it became obvious why. Let's just say people are a little frugal with the truth and don't mention small matters like being morbidly obese or claim to be fifty but look seventy. One assumes a little poetic license is *de rigour* on describing one's self and attempting to make yourself appear as alluring as possible. I had however not lied about my age and a photo can't lie – that is of course unless you have posted a photo taken twenty years previously. That was another little trick which the men employed. Perhaps they were hoping anyone they eventually met wouldn't be very observant and fail to notice that the man in the profile picture didn't quite match the flesh or the age so to speak. How do these people get away with it? You can imagine the scene – going off on the first romantic holiday together and the dreaded passport screaming "Look at me, look at me!" Hmm! The truth will out.

Despite the fact that a number of the profiles were supposed to be my perfect match, on closer inspection it was enough to make you want to be celibate for life. Eventually I settled on a guy who sounded genuine, honest, funny and what's more he posted a photograph which happily tied with his description. No need to check the passport then!

I don't know why humans find the whole dating business so complicated. After all, animals are so much more straightforward. Think of dogs. A quick sniff of the nether regions seems to suffice and romance is full on. No need to enquire about interests. Oh yes… I like walks and adore eating out… bones are my favourite. As for fish, who knows? Do you think all their preoccupation with bonking is preceded by serious amounts of wooing? I can't say I have witnessed any obvious wooing going on in my fish tank but for all I know it could be full on Chateau Algae and a romantic meal *a deux* behind the coral.

Anyway after various e-mails I agreed to meet my date on a Sunday three years ago down by the local canal boat marina thinking a walk in a public place would be a good starting point.

My two boys were at a rugby match and my daughter was at a sleepover. About fifteen minutes before the appointed meeting time I had one of those bang your head against a brick wall OMG moments. I had no car. I had completely forgotten in my nervous anticipation of meeting Nigel that I had left my car at a pub/restaurant the night before and caught a taxi home. I frantically tried to call on my mobile to explain the situation but it went straight to voicemail each time. Then it dawned on me that there was no mobile reception at the marina so all I could do was leave texts and profuse voice mail apologies. Eventually I did hear back as the poor bloke had started to drive home thinking he had been stood up. To cut a long story short he drove to my house (so much for meeting in a public place) and we met on the drive at ten a.m. on the 10th of the tenth month 2010 which I considered to be auspicious. The rest is history and we have been together ever since.

CHAPTER 15

MAD HOUSE

We may be together but it's a mighty complex situation. And without doubt that is probably the biggest understatement of the year. Of my life. You see I haven't *quite* got around to telling my parents that I separated from James nearly four years ago. Unbelievable but true. In fact even my sister Debbie is not *au fait* with the situation. Distance is my ally in that respect. It's not all cloak and dagger. Gill is and always has been fully in the picture and supports my decision, for which I am grateful. Caroline, my sister who lived in Spain is sadly no longer with us, dying rather tragically sixteen years ago, but having a rather wicked sense of humour she would have found the whole thing very amusing had she been around. Not that the situation is funny. Complicated and challenging more succinctly sums up my crazy world.

You see my father is now eighty-seven and declining fast. He remembers yesteryear with an acute accuracy but can't tell you what he had for breakfast and certainly couldn't cope with my bombshell secret. As for my mother, she has enough on her plate dealing with my father so I decided it was kindest to say nothing. If they knew, they would worry incessantly. The fact that we are geographically located a good few hours away certainly helps. I know they won't ever just pop by for afternoon tea to see us. Phew! And now that my father is no longer driving I feel pretty safe. My mother has threatened to get behind the wheel again but so far has only ventured as far as sitting in the car in the driveway and clinging to the steering wheel. One assumes she expects all her long abandoned driving skills to osmotically come back to her. At the age of eighty-two I have diplomatically suggested that driving is best left to the bus or taxi man. That makes me about as popular as a snow storm on a Caribbean holiday, but such is life.

Luckily other aspects of my life are a great deal less complicated. My kids get on very well with my partner Nigel and so does James. We all share the children, even James' dog, spend Christmases and birthdays together, have keys to each other's houses, and ridiculous though it may seem, the arrangement works. Conventional we may not be but mine is a mad house.

Admittedly my parents do find it rather odd that James no longer visits them but they have chosen not to delve too deeply. Thankfully. I think my mother probably suspects but as long as she sees me and her grandchildren, all of whom are happy and doing very well at school, she lets sleeping dogs lie.

As I only see my parents three times a year, it makes my bizarre situation just about manageable… just! Fortunately, we are all adept at remembering what and what not to say, and most conversation usually flows around the children and what they have been up to. Nobody needs to lie, but you can be sure, we are mighty frugal with the truth.

I admit I don't like placing Gill or the kids in such a compromising situation – and on a selfish level, I know my life would be a whole lot easier if I revealed all. However, life is rarely black and white… Or simple.

As for Debbie, well, when I went to New Zealand there was quite enough catching up and getting to know her again without the "By the way" conversation. Not that she would condemn me. She also knows only too well how life can change suddenly and irrevocably.

A lot of things can happen in life in a short space of time. Debbie decided to emigrate to America in 1976 with her first English husband, Adrian, when I was just thirteen. The next time I clapped eyes on her was in 1981 in Helsinki, Finland as she was visiting mum and dad. I had just finished my A-Levels and gone to join my parents who were nearing the end of their posting with the Foreign Office. I had obviously changed and grown up a great deal in the intervening five years. She on the other hand hadn't changed a huge amount, apart from the acquisition of an over the top American accent. She had also acquired a new Canadian husband Brian and a daughter, Charlotte, who was eighteen months old. All a bit surreal really. She divorced Brian many years ago, so she is already ahead of me in the husband stakes and may well understand my predicament. There is however a time and place for all news, whether good or bad, and I shall wait for a more opportune moment to give my "Guess what?" speech.

And who is to blame for this crazy situation? Me ultimately, but it is always useful to have someone else to blame. We do after all live in a blame culture. Somehow or other nobody is ever accountable for their own actions any more. Every time you pick up the paper there's some ludicrous story. You know... some teenager falls in the snow in six-inch vertiginous heels having drunk most of the local pub dry and sues the local council for letting it snow and not warning her about the perils of high heels, or the fact that drinking too much may cause you to fall over. I rest my case.

Most people I know who have a dog tend to blame the dog for all and sundry. If anything is missing, obviously the dog has taken it or eaten it. If someone farts everyone casts an eye of suspicion and disapproval at the dog. This reminds me of a local Conservative party social fundraising evening held in one of the local villages some five years back. All the guests had gathered in a fairly grand private home with a large, impressive *Gone With The Wind* staircase to listen to the local councillor give a speech. The person in question had rather pompously posed half way up the stairs with his impressive gut thrust forward for all to regrettably see and commenced his speech with great aplomb. Unbeknownst to him and the guests the house owners' dog was a serious serial farter. And I do mean serious. Gas masks would have been appropriate but people of a certain ilk do tend to be terribly stoical in times of crisis, and God forbid they would let a barrage of farts spoil the evening.

You may have gathered by now that my family embraces a certain eccentric, off the wall lifestyle. In essence we are not normal or at least *I am not normal* and don't subscribe to the behaviour of your everyday type of person. A pity that I don't own a dog to blame for mishaps and my world of conundrum, albeit I do share James' two-year-old working Cocker Spaniel called Crumble who is an absolute poppet. She comes for occasional sleepovers and we are besotted by each other. So much so that the kids believe I must have been a dog in a former life. Regardless, I could not possibly apportion blame to her for any misdemeanour, no matter how great.

In the absence of a dog there are Creatures. And what are Creatures? For those in the dark this is a generic term we use for all the soft toys which live with us and have done for a number of years. Not just any old soft toys – no, these are special.

There is Brown Bear – yes, I know not very original – who was given to Jocelyn when she was born by her godfather. A bear full of character who has got up to a great deal of mischief over the years. If the cookie jar has been raided we know who to blame. He has recently acquired a girlfriend Tallulah, a funky bear with a purple rinse given to me by Nigel one Christmas. Tallulah now wears one of Jocelyn's baby dresses which she wore when she was only six months old. Quite a lazy bear, prone to promising to make tea etc., but never delivering the goods.

Then there is Kangy. You guessed it – the resident kangaroo, who joined the mad house when my twins were born. Now in the absence of a dog to blame we always blame the kangaroo for anything that goes wrong. He remains stoical in the face of adversity but does get a little peeved when we constantly threaten to sell him when finances are short. Let's face it, such a unique creature would raise large on the open market.

The moose is a whole different ball game. He came on the scene as a Christmas present for Hugo when he was eight and has proved to be a font of all knowledge. There is not a thing he doesn't know and he has dipped his antlers into most professions, or so he says. If ever we have a question to ask or don't know what to do, I can assure you the moose is the first port of call.

Then the rat. Small, but also a major asset. He arrived with a monthly animal magazine as a seventh birthday present for Hugo and is much revered for his talents in the drains department.

And finally there is Lewis. Now if you think we are all mad, Lewis the bear was left as a gift by guests who stayed in our house for The Silverstone Grand Prix. I had previously run a B&B which they had regularly stayed in for the annual event. When I separated from James they came to stay in my new house. Lewis was left with all the other Creatures with a little note to say they knew he would be very happy. Indeed!

You would be surprised how many people have embraced the Creatures over the years. The kids used to resolutely believe they were real. Probably something to do with the fact that I used to move them around the house and have a paw in the cookie jar when they got back from school. But painters, plumbers and others have played the game which only goes to show there is a bit of child in everyone and we should all learn to embrace it. Even now all these years later, the kids know the Creatures aren't real; we know, but it's just a bit of fun and can help lighten life if you let the world of fantasy in.

Oh and I nearly forgot Beary, strangely enough also a bear. Up until recently I had no memory of where he had come from. All was revealed in New Zealand however, as one day I found myself looking at the spitting image of him – a positive twin. The bear was sat on a window seat in Debbie's consultancy room with a menagerie of other soft toys. It was indeed the brother of Beary.

My sister's workspace is quite strange. She is a psychologist but deals with quite a few children, hence the toys. She is also the proud owner of a sandpit which she uses to analyse her patients. On a large shelf she has literally hundreds of inanimate objects – plastic animals, cars, flowers – you name it. Apparently one can determine what course of action to take or treatment to give depending on what objects are chosen by each respective patient to put in the pit. Call me cynical if you will but I am less than convinced. One patient apparently chose nothing to put in the pit and that meant he was going to be OK. Oh really? What a load of...

CHAPTER 16

WORK ETHIC

Mind you, who am I to comment on an area of expertise I know nothing about? Work is a funny thing and one man's meat is another man's poison. Debbie initially trained as a nurse and went on to become a health visitor before moving to America with her first husband for thirty years and retraining. Nursing would not have been for me, although I have a definite penchant for medical dramas and love to try and diagnose patients' symptoms before all is revealed. Strangely I have an uncanny success rate much to my kids' amazement, so they feel convinced I must have been a doctor in a previous life. As I also must have been a dog according to them, because I have such an affinity with our canine pals, despite having avoided them like the plague in my younger years, I've obviously led some pretty diverse former lives. Actually I believe that I was French in a previous life as sometimes I dream I am speaking fluently. A pity this skill alludes me in my present life, although I can certainly get by when holidaying in France and quite like practising on the poor unsuspecting locals. And I can proudly say that I have not yet had to resort to the oh-so-useful 'He is a priest' conversation killer in any language.

My sister Caroline also ended up in the medical profession after her time running the bar/restaurant in Spain. She went on to get a Masters in Mental Health and as she was fairly whacky herself I expect she was well suited to her job. My eldest sister Gill ended up teaching French and now runs a successful after school language club in Winchester. She has the accolade of being fluent in this life. Perhaps she will be a dog in the next life. Who knows?

For myself I have pursued a number of paths. My first Saturday job was working in a coffee house which sold endless pretentious sounding coffee bean varieties. It became clear early on that the general public couldn't differentiate one from the other, let alone know the distinction between caffeinated and decaffeinated. Invariably we would run out of the most popular one and so really any old one would do when rushed off your feet, and no one ever said a word because no one noticed. They did notice however if the cake portion size was on the frugal side, which was a bit of a problem as the manager pre-cut the cake into slices. The number of times I was shouted at by some old biddy who obviously thought I was being mean and abstemious with my cake allocation. One accused me of keeping the extra bit she thought she was entitled to for myself. Ironic really as I'm not keen on cake and more of a savoury girl. Let's just say I didn't enjoy the job very much and the staff perk of being allowed some cake at break time didn't set my pulse racing either.

During my year off after A-Levels I successfully secured a job as an au pair in Switzerland. By some quirk of fate my sister Caroline in Spain contacted me the same week to ask me to go out and work for her, so I did. I thought I was going to be a waitress but a dog of all trades was a far closer description. I cooked, waitressed and served behind the bar, cleaned, did food preparation and anything else, which meant the day was long and knackering. I survived and somehow managed to do a Margaret Thatcher and kept going on a mere four hours sleep a night. Admittedly I didn't work twenty hours a day but it felt like it, and I used to drag myself off to the nightclub after work with friends dreaming of sleep. If I didn't go to the nightclubs I would find myself ensconced in a transvestite bar from two in the morning which my sister and husband seemed to enjoy patronising although God knows why. Some of the male staff had undergone semi-sex-change operations so it was not uncommon to find yourself conversing with a large pair of nipples poking through a man's string vest. So very fashionable you know! As for the makeup… the concept of less is more seemed to pass them all by and I could only imagine how long it had taken to trowel on the foundation for that subtle 'I'm a woman really' look. Many was the night I spent there until closing time at four am, which meant precious little sleep before having to be up for work the next day. Still I'm sure it was all character building. It was certainly a big eye opener after my somewhat sheltered previous years incarcerated in a Victorian boarding school.

After my year off, university beckoned in 1982 and with it the need to land a holiday job to keep me solvent. I pity the poor students now with their student debt looming larger than some countries GDP. Things were different then. You could go to university and have a good time. A good time being a euphemism for spending an inordinately large amount of time socialising without the prospect of future bankruptcy. You literally could have your cake and eat it.

My first job offer was with the Post Office but my father was having none of that. He was convinced I would wear out all my shoes plodding up and down delivering post, so I resorted to being a petrol pump cashier. Until I had done that job I had mistakenly believed I liked the smell of petrol. Mistake. Big mistake. No, even fetid wet dog would have been preferable after a few weeks sniffing those fumes, but needs must and I soldiered on earning the princely sum of £1.80 an hour. People mostly paid for their fuel in cash but 90% of those would end up going a penny over the round number of pounds. If you asked for the extra penny everyone laughed at you and walked off. A penny in itself is neither here nor there but if hundreds of people short-change you by a penny it all adds up. I would sit and stress at how much the till would be short and sometimes naively put in some of my own money at the end of a shift to redress the balance. Not very sound financially especially as I was hardly on a lucrative income earner but what could you do? I could hardly wrestle the offending customers to the ground and mug them for a penny could I? The other bugbear was the number of, one can only assume, pre-menstrual hysterical women who lacked the marbles to dispense the petrol. Despite the fact that it clearly stated on the pump that the button had to be pressed *before* removing the nozzle you can't credit how many muppets failed in this simple task. I lost count of the ranting rages of "I've pressed, I've pressed!" I concluded that pastures new were required for my sanity and luckily landed a job as a doctors' receptionist in London.

In fact there were two surgeries, one at Earls Court and one on the Fulham Road. So I spent my time rushing between the two fighting crazy London traffic on my bike. Now this was a lot more down my alley. Interesting and far better paid and I was able to stay with a friend's mum in Richmond, so accommodation was sorted. Those were the days when doctors handwrote medical notes and the receptionists had to file the cards away which meant it was virtually impossible not to read all about the consultation. That is of course if you could decipher the doctors' handwriting, which at best was illegible and akin to monkey scribble. When I first started the job I considered its location to be very convenient. The surgery was positioned next to a fish and chip shop and in the early days it was handy to nip in at lunchtime for a few naughty chips. In hindsight it was anything but convenient. You do not want to begin to know how nauseating that smell is when subjected to it all day. I began to think I seriously needed a job which didn't have a smell association. Still smell or no smell, I earned some good money and liked the people I worked for, so it could have been a great deal worse. And looking on the bright side, the pungent smell of fish and chips did help disguise the smell of some of the patients who were, shall we say, less inclined to weary themselves with the etiquette of personal hygiene. After my stint as a doctors' receptionist I finally graduated in 1985 and joined a major high street bank's graduate training programme. But before that I had a well-earned holiday with a university mate.

CHAPTER 17

HOLIDAY BLUES

I have found over the years that whenever you enquire about somebody's holiday they invariably reply that they had a brilliant time, the weather was marvellous, the food superb, the people friendly and so on. Now this is either true or they have short memories or low standards, or just can't bring themselves to be honest. It's a bit like when someone asks you how you are. How many times have you said "great" or "good thanks" when it is patently untrue and you have been suffering with the *Bubonic Plague* or even worse… Man Flu. I know we Brits tend to be stoical, much like the family kangaroo but I have categorically had holidays which were far from bliss and warrant a decent post-holiday blues moan.

Take for example my pre-banking career holiday to Spain with my university friend Miranda. When we arrived we caught a taxi and were allegedly dropped off at the stated address. But nothing could have been further from the truth. There we were in the early hours of the morning, totally lost and with not a clue how to find our accommodation. Not to mention not a taxi in sight. If it hadn't been for an elderly couple sitting on their balcony who heard us discussing our "OMG, what are we going to do now?" moment, we would have been well and truly stuffed. They amazingly offered to let us stay the night for which we were overwhelmingly grateful. That mini crisis under our belt at least the weather was really good but I was so busy sunbathing that week, I forgot to drink enough water and ended up with a chronic case of *Cystitis*. If you haven't experienced the delights of this medical condition then count your blessings. It feels like your bladder is on fire and just for good measure it hurts like hell when you go to the loo, so not to be recommended. To cap it all, Miranda contracted a nasty case of prickly heat and was beside herself and in no mood for nightclubbing or anything really. And for the *pièce de résistance* my travel company went bust and I had to pay for another flight home, so all in all not a howling success. It did however cause a few friends to howl with laughter when they heard what had happened.

My main problem when going abroad for that much coveted, much anticipated holiday has been the absence of sun. I have had a number of sun-free holidays in places which were definitely meant to be sunny. Take for example the Dordogne in France. That is without a shadow of doubt meant to be hot and blissfully sunny in July. But the sun decided to pack its bags and depart for pastures new when I arrived with James, complete with rented Citroen and French baguette strategically placed on the rear shelf. Being a typical optimistic Brit I had only packed summer clothes anticipating searing heat and pleasing French cuisine. Instead it poured with rain and was positively cold. At least everything else was good about the holiday, but it is a little difficult to enjoy yourself fully when you feel and look like a sodden rat most days.

Talking of sodden, quite a few years later we were back in France visiting the Loire Valley, this time with our three young children. The twins had only really been walking for a few weeks so were like a pair of skittles falling over all the time. Despite the fact that the weather was horrendous we decided to go to an outside theme park to distract ourselves from the lack of family *joie de vivre*. The boys were as usual strapped in their double buggy and Jocelyn clung onto the pram as if she feared she might wash away. Bearing in mind the deluge coming down on us it was quite feasible we could all have drowned, but we soldiered on for a few distinctly wetter than your average bath hours.

There wasn't much you could do about the weather which remained resolutely bad for the week, but we had major problems with the accommodation, too. The very compact sitting room had some very steep, open tread stairs leading to the first floor, which of course were like a moth to a flame for the children. So we attempted to barricade the stairs with some of the furniture, which of course only made the whole climbing experience so much more fun and dangerous. It's times like this when you wonder why people with very young children think holidays are for a rest. Let's be frank, they can be exhausting and it is possible to go home more weary than when you set off.

I suspect the key to success is to be a bit more circumspect about the glowing details pertaining to your potential rental property. For 'compact sitting room' interpret this as 'can't swing a hamster, let alone a cat.' Then you will not be under

any illusion about personal space and much more inclined to embrace that 'cosy' atmosphere.

To be fair not all my holidays have been soggy, disastrous affairs. Some have been deliciously hot but dubious for other reasons. My first holiday to Gran Canaria with the family some seven years ago started off with a less than pleasing six hour flight delay. Not that any flight delay of any duration is pleasing but if you are adults you can at least find some bar and drown your sorrows as you imagine those wasted sunbathing hours. Children are not so easily placated, and six hours feels like six years when you realise after forty minutes that you have looked at everything the airport departure shops have to offer and have a challenging time void to fill.

When we did eventually arrive at our apartment/hotel resort it was just before nine at night and we were given about thirty seconds to throw ourselves down the canteen stairs before it was too late to eat. Suitcases were abandoned in our frantic haste to find food and drink. On reflection our enthusiasm was a little misguided. The food can at best have been described as barely edible, and bearing in mind I went to boarding school, where you learned to eat anything, this gives you an idea of the gastronomic delights on offer. As for the wine… It very nearly removed the enamel from my teeth and I found myself facing the prospect of becoming teetotal under duress. And if you thought things couldn't get any worse you would be wrong. Oh yes, the accommodation was in a league of its own. I have no recollection when doing the holiday research of any mention of the provision of a bath with the added surprise of no plug. Perhaps they were trying to save water or perhaps plugs were deemed to be extras on top of the all-inclusive package. I'm not sure they really anticipated any of their guests washing during their holiday either as the towels bore an uncanny resemblance to flannels. Bearing in mind the average guest was larger than the average bear I don't think the so-called towels were quite up to the job. Nor do I recall any reference to the downstairs WC being a particular feature; complete with *eau de* sewer fragrance. As for the sliding patio doors, I'm sure they did have the capacity to slide, but you needed the strength of three elephants to achieve this feat. All in all we were *delighted* with our chosen holiday package, especially as it had cost an arm and a leg. If the sun had not shone prodigiously on us I might have succumbed to death by their wine, but thank heavens all was not lost.

We were approached one day by a timeshare rep, which under normal circumstances would have had me running faster than Flo Jo, timeshare usually being synonymous with 'avoid like the plague.' It is a measure of our holiday desperation that we agreed to spend a day at Anfi Del Mar, which turned out to be a top European timeshare resort. It was so aesthetically pleasing in every way that we moved there for the remainder of the week and bought a floating holiday week in perpetuity. We have had some brilliant holidays there since, and it just goes to show there is a cloud in every silver lining.

CHAPTER 18

ONLY MAD DOGS AND ENGLISH MEN

I'm not sure that adage is entirely true in the case of my last holiday, coincidentally to Gran Canaria but not to the timeshare. Nigel and I were in desperate need of the sun especially as the last holiday he had enjoyed was July eight months previously when we had visited Portugal with the kids for ten days. As for the rest of summer at home... the British sun had put in a dismal performance and our BBQ had been lured out of hiding in the shed on only three occasions. Thankfully I had at least been to New Zealand for a break the following January, although it was nothing like your conventional everyday holiday. Debbie had a whole load of tasks waiting for me which kept me gainfully employed. Garage clearance, gardening and bird table repairs to name but a few.

Anyway, Gran Canaria beckoned but I had been unable to book the timeshare as James had planned to take the kids there later in the year. So Nigel and I settled on a 4* all inclusive, adults-only hotel which meant no cooking and no trips to the supermarket. Just total rest and relaxation. The start of the holiday was auspicious enough – the flight was on time – just the ticket to put you in holiday mode.

We woke the first day and I was anticipating blue skies and that wondrous yellow blob in the sky but was greeted by heavy cloud with an ominous look of permanence. Still, what's a little cloud when you've flown all those miles? It was only eight am and it could easily burn off. It could but it didn't and just for good measure a cold wind meant even the most determined sunbathers were sat fully-clothed looking rather frozen. The irony is had the weather been like it at home it would not have crossed your mind to go cloud bathing. But the Brits around the pool and the other nationalities had come for the sun and they would not be easily thwarted.

The second day we woke to a howling gale and twenty-foot waves but still the sun-seekers went and put their towels out to be assured of a prime position. In fact, some of the Brits were so keen and ludicrously early they virtually needed a torch to see where they were going. And to think we laugh at the Germans for being overzealous. I must admit that when it began to rain and people were still glued to their sunbeds I thought they had taken the stiff upper lip a bit far. I say rain but torrential tropical storm or even hurricane would be more appropriate, as the entire island was battered, the hotel leaked profusely and water poured in from every ceiling. Nothing like a good flood to cheer you up. Finally the sun-seekers conceded defeat and were to be seen imbibing hot chocolate and vats of alcohol to warm up. The next day things had calmed a bit, so the more staunch were once again ensconced by the pool, clutching their English newspapers, still sat in a gale.

I can't help but wonder why holidaymakers feel the need to read the depressing home news while they are away? Isn't it bliss to forget the turgid politics and banal celebrity gossip just for a week or two and really switch off? Still, each to their own. I for one can survive without the knowledge that Jordan has had another boob job or that interest rates for savers have plummeted so low that the mattress becomes a viable alternative.

Usually when I am abroad I demonstrate skilled lizard-like qualities which involve lying still and soaking up the sun. As the sun was being slothful and refusing to come out we were determined to still have a good time and enjoy the entertainment in the evenings. Off to the disco it was, but that was my undoing. Whilst I energetically bounced around on the dance floor, I might add totally sober, I suddenly felt a horrendous pain in my left calf and collapsed to the ground. Nigel assisted me off the dance floor with me hopping on one leg and clinging onto him for support. We went to reception to get help and a doctor was called. We returned on instruction to our room but halfway there I fell to the floor. And just when you thought things couldn't get any worse, they did, and in a monumental way. Nigel bent down to pull me up and his back cracked and he collapsed in agony. This was proving to be a holiday not for the faint hearted. To cut a long story short I crawled and hopped to try and get help which was not forthcoming until the doctor arrived forty minutes later. We were both then taken to hospital forty-five minutes later again, in an ambulance, where we spent a number of hours being X-rayed and assessed. Nigel had a herniated disc and I had torn all the muscles in my calf and badly damaged my Achilles tendon.

At least you can't accuse us of doing things in half measures. In for a penny, in for a pound, I always say.

After my credit card had been liberally raided by the ambulance team and the hospital who had both refused to accept our insurance documents, we were left up the creek without a paddle. Or in my case without crutches as I was dispatched back to the hotel and left to crawl to my room. As I had been wheel chaired to the taxi from the hospital in no fit state to walk, I cynically pondered whether the medics thought I might experience a 'eureka, I'm cured moment' just as I arrived back at the hotel. Chance would be a fine thing, as I ended up on crutches for weeks and limped for months afterwards.

The remainder of the holiday was spent with us moving about like two ancient crones hurting more than was tolerable despite being prescribed more drugs than the average chemist dispenses in a year. An old discarded pair of crutches left by a previous hotel guest became my saviour and gave me some mobility, thankfully. The prospect of having to crawl everywhere was less than appealing.

When all said and done it was quite a memorable holiday and a sense of humour was a definite must. It is always best to try and look on the bright side of life and embrace the mantra, 'the glass is half full.'

CHAPTER 19

TROUBLE

An optimistic outlook is all very well but not always easy to maintain, especially if life does not take the straight Roman road. Indeed my life's road has had no respect for straight lines and I have found myself on a long and winding path and precipice with no rope to catch me should I fall.

My life six years ago was the stuff of a Joanna Trollope novel. Everything imploded, including my marriage, admittedly my fault on account of my mid-life crisis. At the age of forty-four my world went a bit pear-shaped. In my case I think an entire orchard of pears was involved. Suddenly I was the talking point of village life, the scarlet woman who had lost the plot. To everyone's incredulity I no longer craved the middle class dinner party circuit. Instead like a Stepford Wife who escaped the cloning process, I rebelled.

I embraced music festivals, live pub gigs and a rather bohemian crowd of people who lived on canal boats, smoked dope, stayed up all night jamming and walked around with scruffy dogs on hairy strings.

This bizarre turn of events meant trouble with a capital 'T' – not just for me, but for my family, too; who couldn't quite understand how their middle class, well-educated mother had suddenly metamorphasised into some rock chic – with a penchant for black clothes, belts and chains.

To be fair, this was not my first foray into an alternative look. I loved the 70s Punk Rock genre; turning sixteen in 1979 meant I lived the era in all its Sex Pistols glory. Whilst my inclination to dress waywardly was definitely limited whilst at home and at boarding school, I was free to express myself at Nottingham University. My persona was unchallenged until I left university to pursue a rather staid career with a leading high street bank, joining their graduate training programme in 1985. Well, at least it wasn't the Foreign Office.

Overnight I had to do a major reassessment of my wardrobe which as you can imagine didn't exactly suggest sensible banker – more Billy Idol. I had a real conundrum as conventionality was not for me.

What are clothes but an expression of yourself and mood? Formal jackets and skirts screamed middle age at me and to be obliged to wear them for my job left me feeling literally like my identity had been stripped away. So what was to be done? I decided that my wardrobe would live a double life. Professional banker – 'you can safely leave your money with me' clothes at one end – the 'real' me clothes at the other end.

Caroline had a similar wardrobe arrangement but hers related to size. Her weight was as erratic as the British weather, and to accommodate the vast fluctuations she had a range of clothes from size ten to twenty! Women talk of having fat days; well, Caroline could by her own admission have a fat month. Still, it always made our irregular get-together moments interesting, as you never knew what to expect. Fat or thin. Even her hairstyle and colour changed with alarming frequency.

Luckily my parents retired to Yorkshire the same month I started working for the bank, a good two-and-a-half hour drive away, so they never witnessed my alter ego look. Probably just as well really, as my father has always been a conventional, conservative dresser. To my knowledge he has never owned a pair of jeans. This you will appreciate is no mean feat and probably worthy of a mention in *The Guinness Book of Records*. How many people do you know who have failed to succumb to the lure of denim?

During the course of my split wardrobe days, I was memorably asked to join my bank colleagues for a social night out. Being a weekend the 'real me' clothes were worn and my hair was punked up with the obligatory entire can of hairspray, dyed with red streaks. Oh, how my father would have approved! Incredibly no one even recognised me when I first walked into the pub, I looked so very different. Of course had my father set his eyes on me I would have been in real trouble, even at the age of twenty-two.

As a child my father was always the disciplinarian. If my mother ever resorted to "I'll be telling your father when he gets home," you knew you were *really* talking trouble.

One particular night, I must have been about seven years old, my father was sat glued to *Panorama*. This programme was the dullest imaginable torture in my childlike estimation. There was only one television in our house so creative, imaginative play was a necessary diversion. Make-believe space adventures were all the rage then as Man had recently landed on the moon,

David Bowie was exciting the pop world with his *Space Oddity* song and the nation had been captivated by *Lost in Space* on the TV. So is it any surprise that I decided, in the absence of any compelling child viewing to entertain me, to dress up as an alien?

In those days my parents owned a rather hideous, plastic, red, conical-shaped vase which sat in a bronze tripod holder with long legs. That screamed antennae to me – perfect for fantasy space travel. Never mind *Panorama* when you could pretend to be an alien. So I discreetly sneaked the tripod back to my make-believe world behind the sofa and stuck it on my head. All was going well until one of the legs broke off. This was definitely an OMG moment and if a spaceship had been passing by I would certainly have hopped on board and happily been whisked away to avoid my father's wrath. In the disappointing absence of such a saviour ship the only solution was to fix the offending item. But not in a subtle, special glue – you would never know it had been broken way. Oh no. I chose to stick the leg back on with Sellotape and strategically placed the vase and tripod back on the windowsill in optimistic expectation of getting away with it. More fool me. My father, who definitely didn't get involved in housework, in any shape or form, was as likely to clean the windowsill and discover my 'crime' as I was to turn into a real alien. However, he did find it, no doubt on account of my mother's overzealous approach to dusting and boy oh boy was I in trouble. No dog to apportion blame to either. Talk about making a mountain out of a mole hill. You would think the finest Ming Dynasty vase had been broken, not some tacky plastic pot.

CHAPTER 20

FASHION

Perhaps the fine red pot fashioned out of purest plastic and aesthetically placed in a 'delightful' bronze effect tripod holder was all the rage at the time. Somehow I doubt it. But there is no denying that fashion comes and goes at an alarming rate both in the home and on the catwalk. This is how retailers become rich and we the fashion victim public remain poor. After all, it wouldn't do if we were all content to wear our clothes until they literally fell to bits or cared not a jot about style or colour fads.

What is it with women's fashion? It changes like the wind and costs an arm and a leg to keep up with. Yet we all obligingly like mindless sheep try to follow the latest trends. Never mind that mint green makes you look like puréed frog or that miniskirts are best suited only to those with a decent toned pair of legs and preferably not worn by larger brethren. A certain fashion blindness descends upon the general public and there is a rush to embrace the frog look if green is deemed to be *de rigueur*.

Admit it, how many times have you succumbed to being a fashion victim? I know I have in the past. Do you remember puffball skirts? I owned one back in the early 90s and it did me no favours at the time but I laughingly thought it looked good. For a start when I sat down all the puff and volume at the back was squashed flat so I would spend my time trotting along the London Underground platforms trying to puff the skirt back to its former glory. The elasticated hem made walking difficult and because my legs were like two stick insects, I struggled to keep the hem at the right position on my thighs for the perfect puff look. So all-in-all not a successful foray into the world of fashion.

My father used to joke with me as a teenager that if the fashion had been to wear a wellie boot on one foot and a shoe on the other I would have obliged and followed the trend. Actually not true, and wild horses would not get me wearing a onesie. Has everyone lost the plot and contracted a severe case of fashion blindness? Why does anyone and especially adults feel the desire to dress up in an oversized baby romper suit? In my opinion they are about as alluring as a bang on the head. Jocelyn owns one, much to my dismay, and it has been banned in my presence much to her dismay. Hopefully as fashion is so fickle this bizarre trend will pass quickly.

As for the latest trend for vertiginous heels, the average giraffe would be threatened by some of the killer heels on sale. The irony is you would probably be killed if you fell from such a great height. Some shoes are so high a ladder has become a prerequisite in order to climb into them. I have attempted to try on a pair of these fashion must-haves and just about managed to stand. The prospect of actually being able to walk in them is quite frankly ridiculous. I shall leave that to the world of celebrities who manage this feat with consummate skill.

When it comes to hair fashion, I confess I have clung to my very long hair for a good number of years. That is not to say I haven't been bold enough to experiment with other hairstyles. At university my nearly waist-length hair was replaced by a short bob which I could punk up and style to my heart's content usually listening to Katrina and The Waves, *Walking on Sunshine* at full volume.

In my mid-twenties I decided to have a perm as they were all the rage. Certainly my salon experience put me in a rage. Regrettably the perming solution was left on too long by my harassed hairdresser who seemed to be attempting to attend to six heads at once, with unfortunate consequences. The result was positively alarming. I looked much like a sheep with a perm which, as you can imagine was neither trendy nor desirable. Another one of life's OMG moments. Luckily I was due to go skiing a few days later so I was able to hide my disastrous coiffure under a hat. To add insult to injury, when I washed my hair it transformed into a frizzy mop, which was worse than the permed sheep look. Radical action was required... and taken. I had the whole lot chopped off and was left a distinctly shorn sheep.

Well-meaning friends sympathised and I was told my hair would at least grow back. Yes, but have you any idea how many years it takes to grow really long hair? As I was no Barbie doll with extendable hair at the press of a button, I had to just be patient and wait. There was the inevitable phase when my hair was devoid of style. In short, a mess. So I resorted to wet gelling to keep it under control until it was long enough to at least be a bob again. Lesson learned.

But when I read in the paper that the short gamine look is the very thing but two weeks later you have to have The Rachel, or acquire super-long tresses that any self-respecting mermaid would covet, I wonder how this feat is achieved. Short of acquiring hair extensions at eye-watering, make your hair fall out in shock prices, I can't see how it is possible to accommodate yo-yo hairstyles.

Personally, I really detest going to the hairdressers and avoid it like the plague. I am known for my cutting edge self-trimmed fringe which invariably leaves me with a unique uneven look. An uneven look is however preferable to the torture I experience when I finally succumb to professional scissors and the dreaded washbasins. Some sadist must have invented those wretched basins. Who in their right mind wants to feel like their neck is being chopped in half? Then there is the added pleasure of some enthusiastic trainee who wants to practise their head massage routine which just leaves me feeling like a load of spiders are crawling over me.

Whenever I wash my hair it remains tangle-free, but not so at the hairdressers. My hair always ends up full of knots which they gleefully attempt to detangle with a comb removing half my hair and scalp in the process. As for the arduous torment of blow-drying… incredibly, I have friends who go every eight weeks for a trim or highlights or some other kind of hair therapy who consider it a relaxing experience. Crazy women!

CHAPTER 21

CRAZY MAD

Mind you, I am considered by some of my friends to be a bit mad and I have certainly done a few crazy things in my time. Take for example the holiday I took with an old boarding school friend to Tenerife at the grand old age of twenty-nine. We were both single at the time and both of us shared a passion for the sun. The only difference was that Dawn only had to look at the sun to achieve a mahogany tan whilst I had to resort to pouring on false tan to avoid the glare of my lily-white skin. We were not alone – there were three others – blokes, whom I had never met, ranging in age from nineteen to thirty-two, so quite a mixed bunch of maturity. Even Dawn only knew one of them and from her description he sounded like a nutter. What possessed me to risk a holiday with three unknowns, let alone share an apartment I shall never know – I guess I was just a little crazy.

Hilariously knowing nothing of me, they had gathered at the airport with Dawn to enquire enthusiastically whether I was voluptuous and well endowed. "Not exactly," was Dawn's reply through snorted laughter. If they had expectations of being ensconced for the week with a Raquel Welsh they were to be sorely disappointed. I was duly nicknamed Miss Ironing Board for the rest of the holiday and we had the most brilliant week, danced ourselves silly at the nightclubs and slept all day.

The following year I found myself flying to Hong Kong on a cricket tour with James who was cricket-mad. I on the other hand was just plain mad to have considered a ten-day cricket holiday when I believed it to be one of the most boring sports invented. However, I did go along with the rest of the team and their long-suffering wives and girlfriends on the most rickety plane I have ever had the misfortune to fly on, which turned out to be some old Russian troop plane. The fact that it managed take off at all was a miracle, considering its knackered state. My seat belt was completely broken and the horrendous creaking and groaning did little to instil confidence. Nor did the sight of a dog which appeared yapping and peeing in the aisles. However there is not a lot you can do once you are on board is there, so you have to grin and bear it, which I did. But I could not bear the thought of using the loos on board so when we gratefully landed in Russia for a refuel I made the mistake of going to the ladies. Finding them proved challenging as there appeared to be a bizarre light bulb shortage at the airport and it was virtually impossible to see. Then just to add insult to injury I managed to lock myself into the loos for half an hour – one of life's less amusing OMG moments. In desperation I eventually escaped by climbing up and over the top of the cubicle wondering why a search party hadn't been dispatched.

And as if I wasn't crazy enough to accommodate one cricket tour, the following year muggins here went on another one, this time to Cyprus. There we were carted around in a tiny white unconditioned van packed in like sardines and nearly bumped off by the overwhelming humidity. A bottle of water could easily be consumed and sweated out within seconds, much to my delight. As for the food, the local meat meze, which everyone else seemed obsessed with, meant that we ended up eating at least three times our bodyweight in meat during the week.

Another holiday in my mid-twenties saw me attempting to ski with eight old school friends in Austria. Fine except we stayed in Hoch Solden which just happened to be situated on a black ski run, which proved to be quite an introduction to skiing. For the uninitiated amongst you this is the hardest run to complete apart from off-piste and not beginners' territory. Unless of course you are mad or at least partially deranged. Nearly everyone else was a competent skier so how crazy was I to contemplate such a holiday? Imagine the scene. I would career down the black slope with zero control, screaming at anyone unfortunate enough to be in my path to get out of the way, much to the bemusement of other skiers, invariably taking the odd one out on my uncontrolled descent, ending up in a crumpled mess at the bottom with a few bruises for my trouble. Skiing was not for me!

I gained considerable notoriety being known as the Crazy Prawn on account of the eye-catching puce pink ski suit which I had bought. It was no fashion statement and worryingly made me stand out in the crowd. When you have inadvertently squashed a number of locals with your skiing prowess believe me, you just want to melt away quietly before they come and get you. And if I thought I had technique problems skiing, even they were exacerbated by poor visibility. Well, how was I to know that I would have balance issues if visibility was poor due to falling snow? Yes, so bad that that I would become completely disorientated and dizzy culminating in me literally throwing up at the end of the run. And this was meant to be fun! OMG! I think not.

My only other foray into the skiing world actually involved a group ski holiday with a twist as there was no skiing by me at all, just sitting and reading. Far safer and a blessing in disguise, I can't help but feel. The reason – I had badly injured my back at the bank where I worked and been carted off to hospital which resulted in me being stuck in bed in agony for ten days unable to even get to the loo without assistance. This proved a little tricky as I was living on my own in London. Luckily for me I had recently met James who lived nearby and he was able to assist me in my not too romantic requirements. When my mother who offered to come and visit to help me heard the situation she nearly passed out, declaring in an obvious flummox that *he* was a *man*, to which I replied that he was the last time I looked! Rather an embarrassing moment, but that's life.

CHAPTER 22

EMBARRASSING MOMENTS

Don't you think life has a habit of presenting unexpected embarrassing moments? I've had my fair share, as no doubt you have too. A number of years ago prior to the departure of my friend *Thrush* I had gone to my GP yet again for help, so he decided for good measure to do one of those delightful internal examinations. Whilst I don't relish these moments any more than being subjected to the obligatory smear test it's all about being a woman and needs must. Generally I don't find these occasions overly embarrassing. After all, a doctor is only doing their job and they have seen it all before. Also in my opinion, once you have experienced the indignities of giving birth there really is little left to be embarrassed about. As for the ridiculous paper towel doctors offer you to cover your dignity whilst they rummage around your bits, why bother? I certainly don't feel any less exposed. Anyway after this particular exposure I was later that evening due to go to a dinner party.

When I arrived my host declared as we briefly chatted in the kitchen that her wonderful GP had been invited. This wonderful GP was of course none other than my own who had seen me in less than flattering circumstances only a few short hours before. As I entered the sitting room cringing with embarrassment he leapt up to warmly shake my hand with an endearing "Mrs Rogers". At least he didn't claim to not recognise me with my clothes on.

When Jocelyn was just seven months old I used to do a bit of child-minding in my own home for a friend I had met on antenatal classes. This arrangement worked well and her daughter Constance was an easy-going child. I had also become firm friends with a woman called Jo whose son James had been born three weeks before Jocelyn. Jo had become pregnant again very quickly and I had agreed that should she go into labour when her husband was at work I would look after James at zero notice. The day arrived and James was hastily dropped off. All was well until I had a frantic phone call from Constance's mum who had an urgent family matter to attend to and wanted me to care for her daughter for a few hours as well.

So I was left with the daunting task of amusing three six-month-old children. To be fair, it probably would have been OK if James hadn't decided to projectile vomit all over himself, Jocelyn, and Constance. All three coordinated their screeches of dismay as I stood aghast at my OMG dilemma – who to deal with first, and was it safe to leave the other two unattended whilst I bathed each of them? Even worse I had images of parents arriving to collect their offspring only to find chaos and their precious ones hysterical and drowning in a sea of regurgitated breakfast. Embarrassing or what?

Fortunately I was able to get the situation under control although my blood pressure took a hammering. I attempted a serene calm look when I returned my charges with some considerable relief.

There's one thing you can safely say about children. They are unpredictable. You never know when your charming, well-behaved child may say or do something to put you on the spot. My parents made the mistake of taking me to a live audience show to see Alf Garnett in Surfers Paradise, Australia when I was ten and at an impressionable age. We arrived at the box office where we were greeted with almost celebrity status as we too were Garnetts, although not related. During the course of the lengthy show I lay across my parents' laps, no doubt giving the impression I was asleep. Nothing could be further from the truth. No, I was wide awake and taking in every crude joke which I gleefully narrated verbatim a few days later to friends of my parents, much to my father's horror and embarrassment.

He was equally mortified when Gill married in 1974. My father was and always has been a traditional man and the sight of Alan her husband on their wedding day left him aghast. A white suit, long hair and an earring in one ear was not exactly the look he had in mind for his son-in-law. The fact that he was actually a rather trendy guy passed him by. He may not have approved of the *ensemble* but they have been married nearly forty years. How time flies.

Tempus fugit. These immortal Latin words were emblazoned on a giant wall clock owned by an old school friend of mine, complete with a fat bulbous fly sitting on the hour hand. The clock lied. Time does anything but fly especially if you find yourself in an uncomfortable situation where every second seems like an hour.

This proved to be the case when I was engrossed in a gardening job some nine years ago. My gardening business developed by default really as I was approached by one of the mums at the kids' junior school. She had greatly admired my garden which was my pride and joy, and often included in the annual village open gardens event. James was equally passionate and green-fingered. Anyway, she asked if I would look after her garden too, and before I knew it I was inundated with similar requests.

On the day in question I was busy removing fallen leaves from a giant pot which had the most exquisite Wisteria growing out of it. The magnificent shrub was enormous and must have taken years to grow. It did, however, have a surprisingly spindly stem for such a specimen, and yes, you've guessed it, the stem snapped clean in half, much to my horror. Definitely an OMG moment. I must confess I was mortified and beyond embarrassed. To my friend's credit she was remarkably forgiving, but then I had always been exceptionally nice to her dog, even if he did make a mess of all the carefully tended flower beds.

CHAPTER 23

MAN'S BEST FRIEND

Other people's pets – you either love or hate them. I suppose it depends to some extent if you have pets yourself as to whether you gleefully embrace all creatures great or small. As I was not brought up in a household with animals unless you count the odd canary, budgie or goldfish I never really felt passionate about anyone's pets. None of my sisters had pets either, except Caroline, whose husband's vile Alsatian was never going to make me a dog lover. It's quite hard to bond with a dog who has shown a propensity to eat family members. My mother has always been terrified of dogs and as a child she would try and hide behind me if an over-friendly one ever approached us. As I was equally keen not to be molested we would turn into 100 metre sprint specialists at the sight of man's best friend. Best friend, indeed! My father and I both suffered the most dreadful asthma if we were around dogs, cats, horses or rabbits. Generally anything hairy. Strangely, if a dog licked me I would instantly become itchy. Furry brethren were not for us.

Have you noticed how animals instinctively sense when you don't want them around? Your friend's cat will insist on wrapping itself around your legs like a second skin and the dog will be over you like a rash. No matter how politely you try to distance yourself from them, not wishing to cause offence, they keep coming back like a magnet and a determination to piss you off or kill you, whichever may be first. I'm sure it is not in my imagination that obsessive pet owners have a clear blind spot when it came to their furry family members.

One dinner party I went to some eight years ago left me thinking it was highly likely I would be dead from an asthma attack long before the starter had even been cleared. The house in question had a complete menagerie of creatures and dogs and cats appeared in every room like they were going out of fashion. The hosts' rather handsome hairy Red Setter took a worryingly clear liking to me and spent the evening tucked up nice and close to my left leg with no respect for my breathing conundrum. The fact that I did not reciprocate his loving advances did not cause him any offence, and I will give him his due, he was as persistent in his amour as the owners were oblivious and blind to my death throes. As I spent most of the evening attached to my asthma inhaler you might think they would have removed their beloved dog, but none of it. In that house the animals ruled. When we first arrived we were offered drinks and then generously told to go through to the sitting room and make ourselves comfortable. All very well, but every seat was occupied by some hairy beast lying supine by the fire, with absolutely no intention of shifting their tails. When an entire cattery and kennel's worth of creatures had been booted off the sofas, we guests were finally allowed to sit. That was the moment I wished I had not made the *faux pas* of wearing black. I find it is such a fetching look to be covered in animal hair trying to look vaguely sophisticated but failing big time.

Years previously when I lived in London one of the couples I used to socialise with a lot had a super hairy, stinky mutt, who would throw himself at you as you entered the house instantly laddering brand new tights and leaving you covered in hair. After several such dinner invite disasters I perfected the art of hiding behind James on arrival whilst he surreptitiously gave the dog the evil eye and hauled it away whilst I distracted the owners with gifts of wine and flowers. As we had met at antenatal classes and I really enjoyed their company I was determined not to let their 'rat', as I endearingly called it, spoil the friendship.

Another friend whom I also had met at antenatal classes had a distinct 'love me love my dog' approach to life. The dog was a boxer and I did not love it – in fact I rather disliked it. It had an unfortunate habit of driving her poor cleaner quite mad with its eating habits. It would wait until all the carpets in the hall had been divested of hair and general mess and then take a large dog biscuit and proceed to munch it and mash it into the clean carpet. Delightful. As for walks with this canine menace, they had to be experienced to be believed. It liked nothing more than to charge up to some unsuspecting innocent park walker and jump up and deposit filthy paws all over them. A number were apoplectic with rage but this washed over my friend, who would gush how her dog just loved them so and wanted to be friends. I can assure you the feelings were not reciprocated.

An old school friend of mine decided that her three children would benefit from being dog owners but of all the breeds she could have chosen she decided on some unidentifiable mutt which, by any stretch of the imagination was not blessed in the looks department. It also slobbered and drooled incessantly, and certainly perfected the art of depositing slobber on me whenever I visited. That made it very popular, as you can imagine.

Other friends had a couple of Spaniels, who are not known for their tight pelvic floor in times of excessive excitement, and the two of them – Pepsi and Shirley – would without fail wet themselves as soon as guests arrived. A charming idiosyncrasy which did much to endear me to them.

Now Crumble, James' dog I must admit has suffered the odd moment of incontinence, as she is want to do when a little hyped up. However, she is forgiven by me, as she is a lovely tempered animal and very loving if a little demanding on the tummy tickle front. Nigel's nickname for her is 'that rotten dog' but I know he is very fond of her really, although perhaps not so when she comes for sleepovers and wakes us all up too early.

Talking of sleepovers the strangest one I ever had as a child involved a kangaroo. I was living in Australia at the time and my school friend had a kangaroo as a pet... like you do. When it was bedtime I was a little surprised to find out we would be sharing a single bed for the night but even more surprised when we had to tuck up with the kangaroo as well. And for the *pièce de résistance* the kangaroo had flees. OMG! So it was a fairly itchy, hoppy night all round and not one I ever repeated. Pets, eh? Where would you be without them?

CHAPTER 24

DOMESTIC GODDESS

Lovely though some pets may be, they can be a hairy lot, can't they and not exactly known for their contribution to the housework? Admittedly some people obviously don't notice or care that there is enough animal hair gathering in their home to stuff several pillows and a mattress besides. If it doesn't bother them why should this bother me? Well, because I am the magic fairy who cleans and tidies and brings order to other families' chaos. I am in fact a Domestic Goddess.

This employment does not please my father, who feels that as I have a degree my skills are being underused and to be a cleaner is not nearly as glamorous as being a banker, which I was for ten-and-a-half years. The irony is that I used to run a B&B which he heartily approved of — one assumes he thought the rooms magically cleaned themselves after guests left. Why *this* cleaning had any more kudos than cleaning private people's homes I shall never know. Perhaps it was the fact that I was running my own business. But even in those days I also cleaned a local pub and was employed in several private homes to keep the dust at bay.

There are benefits however — as I am self-employed I can choose who and who not to work for (bliss) and the hours have fitted in well around school runs. No need to put up with an odious boss and I don't have an in tray to keep me awake at night. Not to forget to mention that you would be surprised how much better paid I am than certain other more prestigious jobs. Not only that but the physical nature of the work keeps me pretty fit too, so no need to pay for sweaty gym membership. All in all, it could be a whole lot worse.

Over the last five years I have met quite an eclectic range of people, some of whom have gone on to be friends. One family I currently work for have nicknamed me their 'posh' cleaner. A few years back I worked occasionally with another well-educated woman and we marketed ourselves as 'Ladies with a Bit of Polish.' Nothing like an upmarket charwoman! Joking aside, you do meet all sorts, so it helps to have social graces and intelligent conversation. It also helps to be a Jack of all trades. I have ironed, cooked, hung curtains, mended things, unblocked drains, de-cluttered, set up paperwork files, arranged flowers, given interior design advice, collected prescriptions and dry-cleaning, decorated, and even gardened. And I have fed a menagerie of creatures and attended to hens, ducks, geese, dogs, cats, horses, gold fish, and even tortoises. I have been a shoulder to cry on, an adviser re finances, a relationship therapist and more besides. Never a dull moment. And as you never know what to expect, it is vital to have a good sense of humour and the patience of a saint. Believe me people can have some very strange requirements.

Take for example the family I used to work for who were fond of spiders. So fond that no spider or web was permitted to be removed. This edict had obviously reached the ears of the local spider population who set up residence with glee in their home. The same rule applied to ladybirds although I didn't find out until I had removed several hundred of them from various windowsills on my first clean. Oops!

But nothing could beat the pedantic bed-making requirements of a man in his nineties I had the impossible task of trying to please. So precise were his demands regarding the placing of the sheets and throws and how they should be tucked in that I nearly resorted to bringing a tape measure and spirit level to work to help me with my endeavours. He even hopped into the bed one day to assess the standard of my efforts, much to my huge amusement.

One family I presently work for own two enormous dogs which are guard dogs in every sense and whilst their names – Mavis and Burt – conjures up images of an elderly, gentle couple, nothing could be further from the truth. Do not be fooled. Definitely a prudent move not to get on the wrong side of them or even pretend to be a burglar. Would you believe it, the owner asked me to meet the dogs and get *their* approval so that I could be comfortable I wouldn't be eaten when I first turned up to clean? I had never had a dog interview before, so it was a first. I arrived for my assessment, trying to look canine-friendly, (whatever that means) praying I would pass muster. The dogs molested me but thankfully in a friendly, if somewhat overzealous, non-eating way, so I passed my interview and fortunately they seem to have taken a liking to me. Just as well, really. Perhaps my children are right and I *was* a dog in a former life. How else do you explain that this canine duo gave me the wag of approval when most other forms of life are if not literally eaten, metaphorically gobbled?

Another one of my clients has a dog who acts as if his tail has been cut off the second he sets his beady eyes on me. His high decibel screeching of canine ecstasy can only be stopped by procuring a treat at breakneck speed – a skill I have honed to perfection to avoid becoming deaf. One could argue he is blessed with canine cunning, as he knows full well one screech is all it takes to win a silence bribe. But not all the dogs manage to fleece me for treats. Why I have such allure to these new found doggy friends is a mystery to me. Despite not being exactly enamoured by man's best friend in the past it is true they have infiltrated my life from an early age.

My first bad dog experience was in Africa when I was six. I had gone to a friend's house with lots of other over-excited little girls to celebrate her birthday. As it was nearly Easter we were all dished out a Creme Egg which I bit into with enthusiastic greedy glee only to discover I hated them. Now I should have just discreetly binned the remainder or politely told the girl's mother that gooey, sweet Creme Eggs were not for me. But oh no, I was too polite or stupid and I can remember frantically wondering how I could dispose of my Easter nightmare and not get caught.

I decided in one of my less smart moments to scoop all the goo out and mash it on the lawn believing that the pet dog would remove all evidence of my crime. I should be so lucky. The dog shared a rather dim view of Creme Eggs and refused much to my chagrin to lick up the horrid mess and bit me when I tried to persuade it to get on with its duty. That was enough to put me off dogs for a good few years. But dogs were not to elude me. My first foray into fundraising as an eleven-year-old in Australia, on behalf of the Adelaide Children's Hospital, resulted in me receiving a book for meritorious service. And what was that book on? You guessed it... DOGS!

Fortunately not all my cleaning clients have pets. They do however have other foibles for me to contend with. An unusual couple of men in their seventies I work for by their own admission, "do own a great deal of clutter." A master of understatement I feel, as their home is a magnet to a vast collection of inanimate objects and enough books to leave The British Library languishing in second place. They also have a penchant for collecting and displaying rugs which are layered and always tasselled to ensure that hoovering is only marginally less onerous than crossing a desert without water. They are obviously oblivious to these cleaning obstacles as domesticity is shall we say, not high on their agenda, given as they are to occupying themselves with impressive intellectual pursuits.

My first visit to their 16th century home for a pre-cleaning assessment left me feeling as if I had walked into the Miss Haversham's home, as narrated in Charles Dickens', *Great Expectations*. Huge cobwebs festooned every ceiling and conceivable nook and cranny. I was assured that they had previously employed a cleaner but as they failed to mention exactly when, I surmised it was unlikely to have been this century! Either that or their cleaner was another spider lover.

After I had cleaned for a good month trying to get the better of the spiders, I discovered by chance a whole new part of the house which I had no idea existed. What I thought was an old latch cupboard door took me up a flight of stairs to another bedroom and bathroom. This totally unexpected find left me in a quandary. Should I admit my *faux pas* or let it pass? I concluded that they either thought I was a useless cleaner as those rooms obviously hadn't been touched by me or they just didn't really notice the difference after I had cleaned anyway. I decided to mention it in a casual way and was assured (much to my relief) that I was not to worry and was doing a sterling job. To while my cleaning hours away at their home I have to listen to their radio which appears to be permanently on, invariably playing opera music or if not some classical *Je ne sais quoi*. Whilst I can entertain some classical music, I abide opera with a passion which is a pity as they are usually in, so I have to try and drown out the caterwauling with my pneumatic hoover. The frustrating thing is they own plenty of great CDs just crying out to be played. If only!

One of my long-standing jobs was with a recently widowed man who was very much at the opposite end of the spectrum when it came to cleaning and cleanliness. Each clean would always be accompanied by a guided tour of each room in the house with pedantic observation of any microscopic dust fibres or dead flies which may have had the audacity to appear since my last visit. He definitely gave OCD a whole different meaning. All cleans were regularly interrupted with, "Stop what you are doing and follow me." Slightly unusual behaviour you may agree, but thankfully not too alarming as such interruptions usually required me to look at some bird in the garden or to be quizzed on my knowledge of certain plants or to contemplate a word in the dictionary. Luckily as I had been a self-employed gardener for three years I proved a match for him when it came to horticultural matters.

I might have guessed he would be quirky as the day I met him I admit I was tempted to never return. Most normal people shake hands and introduce themselves but not this man. Oh no he was different. He was standing by his stables with a very large deranged-looking black Labrador who looked certain to eat me should I be foolish enough to get out of my car. I was beckoned out however, against my better judgement, and told to stand in the corner which I did with incredulity whilst he remonstrated with the mad mutt. When the considerable bollocking was over he came towards me and said, "There can only be one master." Indeed! Despite the odds we did get on well together and I became used to his oddities and weird eating rituals, which often involved me tasting certain foods and meals he had concocted. It takes all sorts!

CHAPTER 25

FOOD, GLORIOUS FOOD

Have you ever been invited to someone's house for dinner or even been at home having a meal and wished you could be a 1000 miles away? Well I certainly have. Peering at platters of questionable cooking and trying to masticate without grimacing *and* partaking of polite chit-chat is a recipe for disaster. Food is such a subjective thing. One man's meat is another man's poison. I confess eating is one of life's great pleasures for me, but not just any old food. That is not to say that only *haute cuisine* will do. Not at all. Nothing like a plate of comfort food such as sausages, beans and chips, when it's cold. The most important thing though, in my opinion is to have the food cooked properly and have it served hot. Cold hot food is yucky.

As a child I tended towards fairly bland, meat and two veg type meals, typical really of the 1960s and 1970s. Let's face it, even salad was dull then. My mother used to put a bit of limp boring lettuce on a plate – God forbid it would be mixed leaves… far too exotic. Next to the lettuce would be plopped a pile of mild grated cheese purporting to be Cheddar, some grated carrot and a slice of corned beef. And if you were lucky you could indulge in a thrilling pickled onion and a watery, tasteless tomato to top it all off. Salad heaven.

My father, who embraced indigestion at every meal time without fail, most certainly did not have the constitution of an ox. He avoided and feared flavoursome things such as onions and garlic with a vengeance. My mother would be berated if excessive flavour sneaked into her cooking, so it was with some inevitability that her cooking was how can I put it politely... plain. My father always said she was a good cook, and indeed she was, but his idea of praise was faint praise at best and he would only go so far as to describe a meal as 'quite nice.' Goodness knows what accolade culinary perfection would have constituted – possibly 'very nice!' Steady on!

Of late he has taken to complaining his food is not served hot enough. Funny how that happens. Especially when a hot plate of food is put down in front of you and at that moment you decide to go off to hunt for imaginary draughts, procure a blanket for your legs and squeeze in a loo visit. It is a wonder that my mother has not seen fit to liberally distribute his meal over his head on more than one occasion.

One of mum's specialities in the 70s was home-made Cornish pasties. As she was born and bred in Cornwall you might think she was on to a winner. Not exactly! If however, you like your pasties dryer than the Gobi desert, then you would have happily queued for these culinary delights, which were never served with gravy. If on the other hand you were not so partial, as two close friends of my parents weren't judging by their facial expressions, Cornish pasty nights were definitely a 'wish you were a thousand miles away' moment.

I don't recall being overly fond of her pasties either but I do have a pasty fetish, acquired as an adult which went in to over-drive when I was pregnant. Most days I would tuck into a cold Gingsters Cornish pasty. Hot ones just did not cut the mustard. Even after giving birth I sat on the ward at about one in the morning tucking into my favourite snack whilst Jocelyn slept, much to the amazement of other new mums. I have even been known to chase a delivery van full of Gingsters and bought one before they were offloaded at the petrol station. How desperate is that?

My mother's repertoire did not stop at pasties. Stew was another stalwart which I detested as a younger child. And woe betide you if you didn't clear your plate to the point where the pattern had been eaten too. Anything not eaten at lunchtime would be presented again in the evening, usually not reheated, for a second innings. Delicious! Nigel's upbringing was much the same – one meal – everyone attended – if you didn't like it, tough – eat it anyway or go hungry. The good old days, eh!

Still I have to admit that it was all good training for my boarding school years where the food was at best inedible but sheer hunger turned it into exotic cuisine through necessity. My boarding house mistress rarely and wisely joined the girls for meals preferring her own delicious looking fare. Believe me I could easily empathise with Oliver Twist who sang of *Food, Glorious Food*.

Having grown up with a rather uninspiring diet it took me a few years to develop my taste buds and experiment with food. When my children were little I despaired that they would never get out of the chicken nugget phase. Thankfully, they finally did but even now, into their teens you are hard pressed to find a complete meal all three of them like. I have become much like

Meat Loaf in his song *Two Out Of Three Ain't Bad*. You get the picture – two like peas, two like baked beans, two like tomatoes and great excitement... three like carrots! Meal times can be challenging.

When I was very young and my godmother, Miss Helliwell, was still alive she used to invite me over to her house to play and occasionally I would have something to eat. One of the wonderful things she introduced me to was pasta in the form of tagliatelle. How I adored a plate smothered in melted butter. Heaven personified. No matter how much I extolled the virtues of the dish to my mother, pasta did not cross our family threshold for many a year. When it finally did I loved pasta so much that I even liked to munch it raw whilst reading a gripping Enid Blyton book. On our way to Australia on the cruise ship, we called in at Genoa for a day where I was able to sample more Italian delights. My father took us to a restaurant where we all had pizza – my first ever – and I absolutely hated it. And yes you guessed it, I had to eat it anyway. No surprise there.

You might think that all this force feeding might have put me off food generally. Quite the contrary – I like eating in or out and I enjoy cooking. That is not to say I haven't acquired the odd dislike. Gazpacho soup is right up there on my all-time 'will never eat it again' list. In fact fried smelly sock would be a more acceptable death by eating experience. You see, I had the misfortune to have this soup at one of my parents' friend's houses when I was eighteen. A pity really because I was too old to pull the 'I don't like it, get out of trouble card.' I'm sure under normal circumstances said soup would be delicious but it's definitely *not* when the host has accidently added double the salt, making the Dead Sea slightly more palatable. Anyway I managed to force my depressingly large bowl of soup down (along with all the other long-suffering guests) only to be asked if I would like some more. Was the woman deranged? Or some kind of sadist in dinner party host disguise? What a shame I had to decline in order to save some space for the main course.

Of course as an adult you have no choice but to grin and bear it, but young children tend to be a whole lot more truthful and are happy for you the parent to cringe in embarrassment as they say exactly what they think of the food on offer. On another occasion the whole family had been invited for Sunday roast to friends, one of whom was a vegetarian. Whilst the wife was no meat eater, her husband adored a good meat roast which she was happy to provide, so I went in the contented knowledge that we wouldn't be subjected to Nut Surprise with lentils and vegetables. Thank heavens. To be fair, she had enquired whether we liked lamb and how we liked it cooked. So whilst there were no guarantees of lamb, I sort of assumed she had got the 'like meat well done' message which I had emphatically conveyed. How wrong can you be? I should have known better when she mentioned her family preference was for on the rare side. Rare! More like raw!

When the lamb finally appeared on the table it was so underdone that it was still baaing, and apart from being devoid of its fleece, this was the only hint that it was dead and had been cooked. Perhaps she had forgotten to turn the oven on, although this was unlikely, as somehow roast potatoes had been produced albeit a poor imitation. Now on occasions like this you want to be sure of catching your children's eyes pretty damn quickly to give them the 'don't you dare say anything' glare. For those of you readers with children you will probably know where I am coming from. I gave one of my quality, turn-you-into-stone glares which seemed to do the trick and convey my angst. To give the kids their due they dutifully sat down and tried their best to eat what was usually their favourite meal but definitely *not* on this occasion.

It just goes to show how important it is for hosts to ask their guests if there are any major food dislikes or allergies and to at least act on any feedback. Mind you I say that but I did have a friend once who warned me she hated any type of offal and guess what my starter was. Pâté. Did I listen? No. Luckily I had an avocado with her name on so quickly rustled up an alternative in true *Blue Peter*, 'one I prepared earlier' style.

Another friend once omitted to mention that she hated fish. It was rather disappointing to find this out at the dinner table, especially as it was mussels and fish for the starter and main. I'm afraid I had to resort to my freezer where I found some sad frozen emergency pie to tickle her taste buds.

I have found myself on the receiving end of many food conundrums. As I have a nut allergy (although not extreme) I am always careful to let hosts know, but you would be surprised how often I have been faced with a nut dilemma, as people forget. So what do you do? What would you do? Should you eat the food and not cause offence but risk death by anaphylactic shock or subtlety pick out the offending items and hope for the best? Or perhaps not partake of the course (usually dessert) with the nuts. The third option works but only if nuts don't sneak into the other dishes as well disguised in dressings or sauces.

I used to know a London couple who without fail entertained at dinner parties with creative delights which always contained pears. Now if I had suffered from a pear allergy I would have been snookered. To be frank I had no idea the humble pear could be so versatile but they positively relished them, and thought nothing of producing three courses with pears in some guise. The inevitability of pears being on the menu used to have me in hysterics with James as we anticipated a 'pearfect' evening and joked that 'pearhaps' pears would be on the menu.

What a pity we lost touch with them soon after moving to village life, as we had a small orchard with plenty of pears we could have happily have passed on.

CHAPTER 26

B & B

When I left London for the country idyll, the house I bought with James had a triple stable set about 100 feet from the main property. The previous owner had not used it in the conventional sense filling it with posh equines but had decided it would make an excellent dumping ground. It was literally filled to the gunnels with every conceivable unwanted discarded item of life. Strangely, a great number of cookery books were dumped unceremoniously in one stable, which on closer inspection turned out to be the owner's mother's books, written by her own fair hand. One can only assume she was not a fan of her cuisine. Perhaps she had been tortured as a child with liver and bacon and was wreaking her revenge. Who knows?

Not wishing to find ourselves dealing with this monstrous pile of detritus we made it clear to the solicitor handling our purchase that the stables had to be cleared prior to completion. Obviously the owner had difficulty comprehending this request as the stables were even worse when we moved in and several skips were needed to clear them. Whilst the owner may have been a celebrity there was no celebrating her behaviour which extended to removing loo seats from the main house on her departure! Odd behaviour in anyone's estimation.

The stables were in a poor state of repair but they were Grade II listed, as was the house. For a number of years they made a good place to store the kids' bikes and toys, gardening equipment and coal and logs. Then we decided to convert them to accommodation. When you leave London it's amazing how popular you suddenly become with friends who fancy weekends away in the countryside. Most weekends we had guests and it started to feel like we were running a B&B so it made sense to create space for friends and family. So we employed the services of a local builder and converted the stables into two beautiful self-contained units, comprising of a private entrance hall with downstairs bathroom and stairs up to a bedroom/sitting room with far-reaching rural views.

One day during the conversion process, I was busy lifting weights to keep fit. At the end of the session I grabbed a big handful of hazelnuts for energy and suffered my first allergic reaction to nuts despite having eaten them all my life with no ill-effects. I literally could not breathe. as my throat swelled and a rash covered my body in seconds. I threw myself into the pantry and swallowed some liquid antihistamine to help suppress the anaphylactic shock and wrote 'nut allergy, get ambulance' on a piece of paper which I thrust into the hand of one of the builders, much to his shock. Fortunately an ambulance arrived very quickly and I lived to tell the tale. After that rather serious OMG moment I have kept a respectful distance from nuts.

Once the conversion was completed it was almost too good to just reserve for friends and family, so we decided to use it for bed & breakfast. This new income stream enabled me to drop my gardening business which worked well around the kids but was a nightmare in the school holidays. As I was clean out of convenient local babysitting grandparents I had to pay to put the kids into holiday clubs whilst I worked. This was a crazy non-economic situation which the stables remedied. At least I could be cleaning the rooms and changing sheets knowing that the children were safe in the main house or garden. Even better there were no childcare costs.

The main issue was how to handle breakfast. I didn't want to get caught up in a cycle of leaping up at some silly hour to produce cooked breakfasts worrying about the merits of fried, poached or scrambled eggs. Nor was this practical with school runs to fit in. So the alternative was B&B with a twist – more Bed and Bugger off! To be fair, we did feed our guests but offered a selection of cereals, wholemeal toast, croissants with apple juice, orange juice, jam and marmalade, all stored in an attractive wicker basket and silent mini fridge. Can't be bad.

Our first guests were friends of friends, which was good. The only problem was they had a dog which they had begged us to allow as they had struggled to find dog friendly accommodation. We had been adamant at the outset that we would have a 'no pet policy' and no children under twelve. Stinky pets and smelly nappies were not for us. Foolishly we relented with the proviso the dog was not allowed in the accommodation. The dog arrived but could easily have been taken for a horse. He was enormous and seemed to suffer from attention deficit syndrome as well as a passion for scaring the feathers off our poor hens, which were traumatised. They were not alone as I watched him thunder around the garden with a disappointing lack of respect for carefully tended flowerbeds. Lesson learned. Stick to your guns.

Sometimes guests turned up very late long after we had gone to bed. To resolve this problem we had a policy of leaving the rooms unlocked so guests could let themselves in, which was convenient for everyone. This meant people sometimes arrived unannounced and had left the next day before I even set eyes on them, just leaving the cash on the side. I had no objection to people letting themselves in if it was very late but a young guy turned up one afternoon without so much as a by your leave, even though it was obvious I was in and availed himself of all facilities. When I went to knock on his door to greet him through gritted teeth he appeared with a small hand towel only just covering his modesty. This added insult to injury as all guests had two large bath towels provided. If he thought it was bed & breakfast with added benefits he was sorely mistaken and my withering glare put him and his assets in their place.

One of our regular guests owned a part share in a canal boat which was moored in a village near to us. Oddly he never chose to sleep on the boat, preferring to spend his nights with us. He never even had breakfast and you would be hard-pressed to know he had been in the room. To be fair, we were very lucky with all our guests who never caused any damage and only showed respect for their surroundings.

One of the most unusual guests was a hundred year-old man who used to visit every year with his son who was in his seventies. He had lived in the village many years before and liked to return for a nostalgia trip. He was an avid and skilled chess player and liked nothing more than putting his skills to the test with me. My godmother had taught me to play when I was just five years old and I had played for my school club but was soundly trounced by this man much to his glee on every occasion. I recently heard that he had died at the ripe old age of one hundred and five, and quite strangely his son died a few months later.

CHAPTER 27

CAREER GIRL

Little did I know when I left Nottingham University that I would one day run a B&B. When I graduated in 1985, I went on the usual milk round to fight and scrap for jobs. After considering insurance as a career choice I eventually decided I wanted to be a banker. Goodness knows why, as nobody in the family had ever gone down that route. However banking lured me and I was lucky enough to be accepted on a three-year graduate training programme with a reputable high street bank.

All new entrants were expected to be flexible and accept that they could be moved to various parts of the country during the training process which covered work experience in three branches and three departments. Now I had no particular affinity with any part of the country, having lived abroad a great deal. I loved Nottingham where I had happily done my degree but to live there as a non-student would no doubt have been very different and not nearly as much fun. The only place I really, really didn't want to go to was Bedford. My old haunting ground for boarding school was rock bottom on my list of desirable places to live and work. So I considered myself to be super flexible, geographically speaking, with one exception which I stated with some vehemence on my application forms (possibly my undoing). Well, better to be honest and not kid yourself or anyone else for that matter. Unfortunately someone at the bank in charge of graduate placements had some warped sense of humour and no doubt thought it highly amusing to offer me Bedford branch to kick-start my new career. This caused a major 'dolly out of pram moment' and I had a big sense of humour failure which served no purpose as the bank was intransigent on the matter.

So Bedford branch it was, which was ironic as I was the first graduate to have ever been trained there and was regarded with suspicion and a degree of resentment. Being fast tracked through all the jobs and being paid more than other staff with years of experience is a recipe for a challenge. Still, I like a challenge so I buckled down and learned a myriad of back office jobs which culminated in cashiering and dealing with some amusing general public. One very ancient lady used to call in once a week and demand that she could count her money. No amount of explanation of the banking system would suffice. She firmly believed her money was kept in a named shoebox and was determined to regularly check it was safe. So we dutifully obliged and her monies were handed over for counting in a shoebox to placate. Bless.

Within a few weeks of starting work I was approached by Personnel Department and asked to represent the bank at the annual Royal Smithfield Agricultural Show in Earls Court, London. What an experience that was. For a start I was hardly a banking aficionado. I had a week's induction course under my belt but my concentration levels had been somewhat tainted by a badly timed severe bout of *Cystitis*. Well, you try concentrating on banking theory when all you can think about is going to the loo! However I did have the gift of the gab and you would be surprised how easy it is to chat away and charm overly imbibed jovial farmers, most of whom had no intention of talking bank or business but were much more inclined to indulge freely of the bank's hospitality. 'Just a wee dram' was a euphemism for a good half bottle of whisky consumed with vigour and much good humour. So my week was hardly arduous and mostly involved making polite conversation, handing out leaflets and generally luring would be customers over to the stand.

My seven months' stint at Bedford passed quickly enough and then I moved to Camden Town, in London where I stayed for a year acquiring more skills under the watchful eye of my manager who shared my surname and was a fun hands on type of man. No heirs or graces – he would happily file cheque books if necessary. He without fail would join all the staff on a Friday night at the pub and we would drink until we were booted out. In those days I had a penchant for drinking pints of lager with a sherry chaser. How weird is that? The staff were a good laugh and the branch location was fantastic with the deliciously eclectic market stalls and bohemian people who were attracted to the area.

Sadly I had to leave eventually and ended up in another branch in London which dealt with high end arrogant customers. I was working on the foreign till one day when a woman swanned up to the counter, banged her hand and screeched "Lire" and disappeared off to the sterling counter. For those in the know and I was not one of them, this was Lady Snotgrass or some other highfalutin name. Her expectation was that she would be recognised and her needs attended to immediately. As I was clean out of crystal balls I didn't know how many Lire she wanted or when. Too bad seemed to be the sentiment and get on with it.

Other challenges arose in the lending department. Terrifying overdraft facilities were constantly demanded by individuals of precious little means but who were titled or expecting to inherit one day. The constant cash-flow required for one's dinner party entertainment never ceased to amaze. I was used to declining requests for overdrafts at the previous branch if income could not support the need but 'no' was not part of this branch's vocabulary and my manager was hugely amused by my outrage at the excesses allowed.

Thankfully only four months later I was moved on again. I say thankfully but I ended up with a two-hour commute each way and I hated the job which lasted a tortuous eight months, during which time I nearly resigned. The pace was so stultifyingly slow in the credit card department where I was incarcerated that snails would have been deemed Olympic potentials. People would fall asleep in the staff room at lunchtimes, no doubt bored to death by the tedium of the job. My escape eight months later was a very happy day in my life.

My next transfer to a department handling the stocks and shares for corporate customers was really uplifting. I was promoted to management and fell in love with the stock market world which was challenging and interesting. For the next seven years I threw myself into my career but then decided that to further myself I would have to join another bank. Besides, the American banks all paid much more handsomely for the global shares skills I had acquired so I approached an agency to find me new employment and started the interview process. By then I had become frustrated with some of my bank's senior management and their policies so took the rather radical decision to resign before securing a new job. Fine, except a few weeks after resigning I found myself pregnant. Unfortunate timing and a definite OMG moment. Still I am not one to overly panic and I did want a family so my working days came to a halt whilst I waited for the arrival of Jocelyn.

CHAPTER 28

DON'T PANIC

As a nation we seem to have recently become obsessed with the wartime slogan 'Keep Calm and Carry On' – these moral boosting words being embossed on mugs, plaques and posters. Indeed I bought myself such a worded wooden plaque when I moved to my present house. At the time in the face of considerable adversity and crisis it was very apt to adopt this life's approach. For those of you young enough to have watched *Dad's Army*, you will recall Corporal Jones imploring Mr Mannering to not panic, ironically invariably running about like a headless chicken, the very personification of panic. Still we Brits are very stoical and no matter how dire the circumstance we are renowned for our stiff upper lip/can do attitude. This has served me well.

The last time I moved house, I was separating from James and starting a new life. The day that unfolded was beyond memorable. Indelibly printed forever in my mind and right up there for a good excuse to have a full-on panic would be my best assessment of a very difficult time. You will recall that my parents were not privy to my marriage breakdown so they just thought we were moving house to facilitate secondary school education. If only it was that simple.

The British weather was true to form and dire as we found ourselves battling with a temperature of minus eleven. My father was at a loss to understand why we had chosen to move in such bad weather as if I could have predicted the severity of that winter. Let's face it if you waited for decent weather, no one would ever move. However, my dad can spend half an hour debating the merits of wearing a vest or top coat versus a rain coat and umbrella when considering leaving the house for a shopping trip so wrapped up he is with the British climate. Luckily the removal men arrived despite the challenge, only to find they couldn't get down the gravelled driveway because there was two feet of snow. This presented a huge problem as the drive was at least two hundred feet long, so not exactly a hop, skip and a jump to empty our home and contents. And we owned an alarming number of things – for a start five double beds, five single beds and six sofas… I could go on. It was so perishingly cold that the kids were running around with coats and dressing gowns just to try and keep warm. Perhaps if onesies had been invented then I might have relented and worn one just to avoid hypothermia. Needs must. And as if the weather wasn't enough to panic the average person, things got a whole lot worse.

To complicate matters our possessions were being split and going to two different destinations – the house I had bought and James' rented accommodation (pending his purchase). James had flitted backwards and forwards to the rental property with a large van, full of a lifetime's collection of smaller items, leaving the big things and heavy furniture to the removal men. As the cost for the move just a couple of miles away was an eye-watering six grand I dread to think what they would have charged if they had transported everything. We probably would have had to sell the furniture to pay them.

As I charged around the house with my hoover cleaning each room as it was emptied, my mobile rang and disaster had struck. Jocelyn had been helping her father offload one of their many van loads when the water tank in the rented property burst and the property was flooded. The property had been empty for some months as the English owners were stuck in France, unable to sell their house, and all the months of freezing weather in an unheated house had finally taken its toll. This was definitely an OMG moment. The house was uninhabitable so we resorted to Plan B – not that we had a Plan B up our sleeve at the time – no surprise there – as who could have imagined such a scenario? Plan B was simple enough. James moved in with me and stayed a week whilst the rental house was filled with dehumidifiers to dry it out. Keep calm and carry on we did and all was well.

If there's one thing I can say about my family and especially James is that they are pretty laid back, not really the panicking variety and prone to take things in life as they come. James is so laid back sometimes that he could almost be described as horizontal. Take for example the day we moved into our countryside home in 2001. The boys were only two and my daughter just four. The removal men arrived with three huge lorry loads of our possessions which took a mammoth task of coordinating, as if it wasn't hard enough keeping our eye on three excitable under-fives. The entrance didn't have a gate when we arrived to stop the kids escaping and the garden was over an acre and the perfect place to 'get lost.' If ever there was a time for both parents to be 'hands on' this was it.

Except James had other plans, having been the proud recipient that day of a sit on lawnmower which was like an all-time dream come true. He hopped on his new toy and calmly in his own seventh heaven cut the grass, which I might add took hours. Boys and their toys. Did I panic? A bit. You bet! Did I show it? No. I am the mistress of appearing calm and internalising stress, so to all intents and purposes nobody knew that inside I was flapping but to be fair the excitement of the day was the overriding factor.

The following day with no grass to act as a distraction (phew) James started to connect up the TVs. As we were unpacking kitchen boxes we switched on the television to see footage of the two World Trade Centres being attacked by terrorists in the USA. At first we thought it was a film until we realised all our TVs and channels were showing the same disaster. This was a very sobering moment as I had visited that very building on business on a number of occasions when I worked for the bank. And the harrowing filming of the ensuing panic and carnage will always stick in my mind.

I also narrowly missed the King's Cross, London Underground fire in November 1987 by only half an hour which claimed thirty-one lives and injured many others. One thing is for sure, you never know how you would react under such extreme circumstance, even if you are not a natural panicker.

Take for example Cyclone Tracy which struck and devastated the city of Darwin, Australia on Christmas Eve

1974. It destroyed seventy percent of Darwin's buildings and 80% of the houses, one of which was my parents' house we had lived in only a few short months before. The family who moved in after we left were saved by the extreme bravery of the husband, a colleague of my father, who literally held up the breeze block walls of a lower ground utility room to protect everyone.

I don't know if everyone's life is full of near misses but I do believe that we all have a time and a place to fulfil our lives and if it is not your destined time to die you will continue on life's journey. Three-and-a-half years ago when I was single, I had a pretty serious car crash which could very easily have ended in my demise. I was travelling to work at seven-thirty in the morning and it was drizzling slightly after quite a dry summer period. Although I was only travelling at forty miles an hour the car suddenly felt like it was gracing a skating rink and I totally lost control. I veered off the road, across a ditch and hit a large tree which flipped me back onto the road. Luckily there were no other cars in front, behind or on the other side. The whole incident probably only took a few seconds but everything went into slow motion and I felt myself succumbing to panic as I wrestled with the wheel. Strangely, when the car stopped I felt oddly calm, put the brake on, turned off the engine and exited the front passenger's door as the driver's door was jammed shut. By then, two cars had stopped some distance from me and I approached one ashen-faced driver who seemed far more traumatised than me to ask in a ridiculously calm way if they had a hazard warning triangle as we were on a blind bend. The car was a total write-off being crushed on most sides and three wheels had become detached. The emergency services arrived and apart from the obvious bruises and some whiplash I was very grateful to be alright if a little shaken.

Two days later I was back at work on my shift at a village pub cleaning, despite my injuries, which goes to show if you are self-employed you jolly well get on with it or you don't get paid. I then had the added pressure of sourcing a new car in three days as James was off to France with the children for a ten-day holiday. So I found myself test driving a new car and having to put all my post-accident fears behind me. I never told my parents what had happened as they would have fretted endlessly. My much loved Vauxhall Zafira, which I had originally bought to facilitate my gardening business as it had sufficient space with clever configuration of the seats to accommodate my children and lots of tools was replaced by a Golf.

I also cheated death in 1997 when Jocelyn was nine months old as I suffered a severe asthma attack. The day had begun innocuously enough – James had gone off to play cricket and I was pottering around at home. Whilst I had always had asthma from early childhood and been hospitalised on a few occasions, as an adult I had managed the condition better. This time was to be different. As my asthma attack started and the symptoms worsened even after taking medication I sensed the situation was becoming serious. James was not contactable so I phoned a local friend whose husband offered to take me to St George's Hospital in Tooting, London. By the time we arrived, fighting heavy traffic on the way, I was in real trouble with my breathing and definitely becoming panic-stricken. In A&E I nearly died and vaguely recall being surrounded by numerous nurses and doctors who were attempting to save me.

People who have described near death experiences make reference to a tunnel and strong light pulling them. I experienced this very phenomenon and very much felt the decision was in my hands to live or die, but to live took a great exertion of will. I chose to live.

CHAPTER 29

MOVING ON UP

I have certainly lived in a great number of homes and places in fifty years. What an understatement! It is said that moving house is one of the most stressful experiences in life, right up there with divorce and death. I must be some kind of masochist because I have moved house more times than a hermit crab changes its shell. Admittedly many of these moves were as a child and not all have resulted in the purchase of property but even so, a move is a move, which imposes change – and change can be stressful.

If you consider my life to date it has been fairly eventful on the moving front. My father's job with the Foreign Office involved an awful lot of upheaval and family and friends were forever in the wake of goodbyes. Foreign postings would last approximately two years, sandwiched by a home posting of shorter length.

I have no recollection of Singapore, where I was born and lived until I was two. I was still too young to recall the next home in Belgrade, Yugoslavia but clearly remember Kampala, Uganda where I attended the local school with my sister Caroline. My first day sticks firmly in my mind, as I wet myself, being too afraid to ask the teacher if I could go to the loo.

England beckoned again before going to Darwin, Australia where we lived in our first house for only six months before moving again to a new build house on stilts. Boarding school junior and senior houses became my new homes after that, followed by a posting to Mbabane, Swaziland which at the time was ruled by King Sobhuza the Second, who was famous for having more than his fair share of wives. My father's final posting to Helsinki, Finland ended shortly after my A-Levels. OMG, ten homes and I was still only eighteen. During my year off I went to live and work in Spain for three months before staying with my parents once again prior to university starting. At least their home in England which they bought in 1964 provided some consistency.

Even university provided no respite from my 'here, there and everywhere life.' Whilst there, I spent my first two years in a student flat just off campus but one term was spent at university in Waukesha, Wisconsin, America and in my final year I moved again to a rented house in Nottingham with friends.

When I graduated I moved, as you will recall begrudgingly to Bedford to start my banking career and rented before upping sticks and going to Finsbury Park, London for a year. Other parts of London lured me – this time as a property owner – Woodgreen, Turnpike Lane and Battersea. When I sold my flat in Battersea in 1993 I moved into James' flat for just four months whilst we house-hunted. The house we found became home for a whole six years – amazing! Then off to Berkshire it was to share Grandpa Robert's home for eight months until we found our cottage in Northamptonshire which was home for an incredible eight-and-a-half years. A record. However, even then I did move out and rent a place for a few months whilst I was having my mid-life crisis. When I eventually separated from James I moved to my present home which has been my new nest for nearly four years. Twenty-five homes in fifty years – not bad going and almost verging on nomadic!

Each time I have bought a property I have immediately embarked on a major renovation project. Not for me outdated kitchens and bathrooms and questionable décor. To be honest I love DIY. My parents on the other hand have lived in their present house for nearly thirty years and the original avocado bathroom suites have survived intact. I suppose if they hang onto them long enough there is a chance they may become fashionable again.

It is surprising really that I have discovered my inner DIY skills and property development enthusiasm as my father was never a dab hand at these matters. I recall him decorating the main bedroom as a child when the fashion was to have rather dreadful polystyrene ceiling tiles. The tiles themselves were not too taxing to fit in place however cornicing was not his strong point, nor wallpaper hanging. He definitely had a penchant for choosing difficult repeat patterns which never matched up when hung under his expertise. Still, my mother never seemed to notice, or at least if she did she didn't say anything. Diplomatic as always – after all, she was the wife of a diplomat.

It's one thing to forgive your husband if their decorating skills aren't quite up to par but if you are paying good money for a so-called professional to do work then it's not unreasonable to expect a quality result, is it? Well that's what I misguidedly thought when I had a loft conversion done in London in 1998. Everybody I knew was craving more space with growing families busting the seams of the average terraced house. Moving house was an expensive business so it was all the rage to extend your home in every possible direction. My sister Caroline had recently and unexpectedly died, and as a result I had inherited some money which meant we could afford to pay for an extension.

One couple James and I knew via NCT classes had already taken the plunge and completed a loft conversion with surprisingly little upheaval and no loss of sanity. So we optimistically appointed some Irish builders who I can honestly say nearly drove me potty over a five-month period while they attacked our home and swore incessantly. Jocelyn was only eighteen months old at the start of the build and at the toddling stage. Not good when your builders decide not to put a false ceiling in to protect your home from all the dust, rubble and elements of the build and kept leaving the front door open so Jocelyn could escape. We had (I kid you not) three feet of rubble outside our bedroom door and water poured in like a river when the roof was removed, and they sailed off for the weekend failing to put up adequate tarpaulin.

Everything that could go wrong did go wrong, right down to the hanging of the wallpaper in the hallway and missing the pattern repeat. They must have known my father! Things became so bad that I resorted to spending time at a friend's house during the day while they were at work so I could escape the mayhem.

One day, however, I decided to stay at the house as there was only one carpenter on site. Jocelyn was having a lunchtime sleep in her cot when I heard a blood-curdling scream. I raced upstairs to find the carpenter had cut his thigh very badly with an electric saw and blood was pouring everywhere. I rushed to grab a belt and put his leg in a tourniquet, phoned for an ambulance and tried to calm the poor man who was in shock, as was I. He was lucky not to have severed an artery and was off work for a long time recovering.

You would think that this would put me off major building work for life but not a bit of it! When we left London for the countryside we had a big extension put on the main house, reconfigured the kitchen and the floor above it, as well as converting the stables for our B&B. As for my current home, within a few months of moving in I had the integral garage converted into a second sitting room but not just any old sitting room – no, this was to become the 'rock 'n' roll room'.

CHAPTER 30

ROCK & ROLL

It was clear from the outset that Nigel and I were both passionate about music. Between us we have gathered a very broad and eclectic range of CDs and LPs over the years with a lot of punk to liven things up, just for good measure. Some of my LPs I have treasured since the 1970s when I first started taking an interest in pop music. Sadly I no longer have a turntable to play them on but they remain carefully stored in memory of a very different music era.

My music taste has also been greatly influenced by having three sisters who are six, nine, and twelve years older than me, respectively. So whilst I was only very young in the sixties, the music from that period seems very familiar. I have the clearest memory of being wedged in the back seat of my dad's car, with my siblings all singing, *San Francisco (Be Sure To Wear Flowers In Your Hair)*.

When I first met Nigel the garage had already been converted but it was to evolve into a room that celebrates some of the many rock and pop icons whose music we so admire.

First, however, we created a rock 'n' roll landing. The house landing is large and galleried and the perfect place to hang framed posters – almost like a museum exhibition of yesteryear music.

We had such fun choosing the posters but really struggled to narrow our wish list down to the available wall space. So we decided to dedicate the converted garage into a further rock 'n' roll sanctuary. With tongue in cheek we have the words 'IF MUSIC BE THE FOOD OF LOVE – ROCK ON' emblazoned on the wall. I trust Mr William Shakespeare will forgive this sense of humour. And amongst the many iconic poster images we have tracked down with considerable difficulty as some are no longer in print, is a beautiful coloured glass framed work of art. Made by my friend Claire and given to me by Nigel as a fiftieth birthday present, it replicates the logo of a local band called Leatherat which I have followed for a number of years since seeing them at the Cropedy festival.

Now being a music lover I have gone to a few festivals in my time but I have come to the conclusion that camping is not for me. My dismal efforts at trying to put up a tent at The Levellers' Beautiful Days festival five years ago left me feeling distinctly un-rock chick. The end result – a rather crooked affair – was an embarrassingly good example of how *not to do it*, and even worse I was surrounded by seasoned and experienced festival goers. I suspect they also had the good sense to secure flat ground for their temporary *boudoir*, which in hindsight I wish I had given more thought to. For three nights I slid relentlessly to the bottom of the tent in a crumpled heap which made the concept of sleeping a little challenging. I ended up looking fetchingly knackered with not so much bags but suitcases under my eyes. Perhaps in future I could cheat and rock up in a camper van. But that would be seen to be giving up, not something I am in the habit of doing. Would you?

Chapter 31

OLD HABITS

I guess we all have habits or little idiosyncrasies which can be endearing or just plain infuriating for other people. They do say old habits die hard and I suppose we are all creatures of habit to some extent. No doubt I have plenty of infuriating habits – my excessive need for tidiness and order generally drives my children to varying degrees of insanity, but then Jocelyn's bedroom which often looks like three bombs have accidently dropped on it doesn't exactly thrill me either, and her assurances that she will tidy up later does little to placate – no surprise there. 'Later' is generally a euphemism for some time in the future but her future could be in the next ten minutes or when I am consigned to a zimmer frame and of advanced years. Mind you, if she thinks I am excessively tidy she should try living with Debbie. She owns an enormous Chinese rug which is hoovered so that all the pile goes in the same direction. It is so perfect that no one is actually allowed to walk on it. OCD or what?

My mother on the other hand has a habit of cutting up her food into fairly small pieces, and then meticulously loading her fork with a bit of everything. Just when you think she is going to pop it into her mouth, she knocks the whole lot off and starts again. And although I find it drives me potty to watch her doing this, I am compelled to watch and can't look away. I made the mistake of mentioning this idiosyncrasy to Jocelyn whose eye I have had to avoid at mealtimes at my parents' house ever since as we both know we will end up in fits of laughter. Just as well we only visit three times a year.

My father is in a league of his own when it comes to irritating habits, but without doubt his ability to suffer from what I call 'draught syndrome' is second to none. If there is a draught, real or imagined, he will sniff it out at a hundred paces and then complain vociferously about it. No one else I might add is ever bothered by similar draught issues, but I have been seated enough times in cafes with him to know that several moves will be inflicted on everyone to accommodate draught-free perfection.

In his driving days he would literally drive me dippy with his dip stick obsession. Any journey, no matter how short had to be preceded by a dip stick checking session and much contemplation of oil levels. I don't know about you but I have never succumbed to a dip stick moment in my life.

On a slightly less savoury note an ex-boyfriend of mine used to have the dreadful habit of removing one sock and picking his toenails when he was on the phone. I don't know if I am just intolerant but I always had to vacate the room on those occasions as I couldn't bear to watch. Well, could you?

Then there was a girl I used to share a dorm with at boarding school who was blessed with an outlandishly large chest. Her bedtime ritual involved beating the hell out of her horse hair mattress to make two wells to drop said chest into so she could lie comfortably on her front. I have no idea what it would have been like to have such a front but she certainly used to put my back up with the drama of the process. Perhaps I was just jealous of her assets.

A similar trick was employed by a humongous man I witnessed sunbathing on holiday some years ago. He was busy for ages scrabbling in the sand digging a large hole when he suddenly flopped on his front and dropped his impressive girth into the pit and was able to lie flat without discomfort. Inventive and hilarious to watch.

Then there was a cleaning job I used to do for a man who was obsessed with catching mice, which did tend to visit his house as he was surrounded by fields. However, he failed to see the irony of his habit of leaving tempting bowls of nuts out for his own consumption which no self-discerning mouse could or would ignore. The mice used to pinch the nuts and store them under his sofa cushions, much to his chagrin.

CHAPTER 32

HOT FLUSH

These things are all relative, however, and his chagrin pales into insignificance compared to mine when I found myself abandoned in Spain in 1982. Yes, abandoned. OMG. Norman decided on a whim of madness to leave Spain unannounced and return to England. You may well wonder why. I have no idea – just barking mad, I guess, like his dog Bimbo. And just to add to the conundrum he took Caroline's passport and all the money. Great!

Caroline was left with little choice but to make emergency arrangements to track him down and I was left to hold the fort. Although how I was meant to run La Panterra Naranja single-handed I shall never know. Luckily for me, by a quirk of fate, the electricity supply was cut off due to an unpaid bill and as there was no money, the problem was solved.

Although I could hardly have declared myself carefree with an absent sister, serious cash flow issues and not a clue how long I would be home alone. True to form, my parents were not privy to my evolving predicament, believing me to be having a lovely time. If only.

Caroline did eventually return two weeks later having found Norman in a mental institution which seemed to justify my assertion that he was indeed as mad as a fruit cake. I might have been forgiven for going a little mad myself under the circumstances, but farcical though my life was I managed to survive the ordeal and returned to England where I regaled my parents with positive tales of my Spanish saga. All this frugality with the truth was enough to put me in a hot flush even at the tender age of nineteen.

Speaking of hot flushes I have recently become one giant, all-consuming, permanent hot flush – a walking advertisement for the menopause. Disappointing and inevitable but at least there is not a hint of menopausal Boobitus. Phew! There are benefits, however. We have just turned off the central heating and now all the family just cluster around me as if I were an Aga and soak up my nuclear thermal excess. Whilst they all acknowledge I am pretty hot stuff – ha ha – and look well, they don't really appreciate that 'run over by a giant kangaroo' feeling, which seems to go hand in hand with my new found broken body thermostat.

Believe me, hot flushes are no joke. Mine can go on for hours, so I can't help but feel it's high time someone invented a way of plugging overheated ladies into the National Grid. Never mind solar roof panels and wind turbines, bring on the women! In the meantime, I have resorted to HRT to cool me down. I am now definitely cooler, which is bliss, but I'm permanently hungry and rather itchy. Still, you can't have it all.

The need to scratch like a baboon reminds me of when I had the misfortune to contract *Chicken Pox* when I was thirty-five, courtesy of Jocelyn. I did look monumentally dreadful which complimented the way I felt perfectly and was quite good for the sympathy vote. I had so many spots that there were spots on top of spots and in places I didn't know they could go. No, please don't ask! Even Gill declared on visiting me that it was the worst she had ever seen me look. You just can't beat a bit of sisterly TLC, can you?

Still, I soon got better and was spot-free for Christmas and ready to take on the challenges of the festive period. Christmas can be a tricky family time, can't it? Trying to please everyone but invariably not yourself. Who to spend Christmas with and who have you offended by not sharing your Santa moments can all become one big headache. And if you don't spend the day at home, you have to do Christmas somebody else's way, which in my experience means being dragged around some cold, wet park for a walk to work off the turkey when you would much rather be watching *Chitty Chitty Bang Bang*. Never mind that you have seen it a thousand times before. Or the obligation to all settle down to the Queen's Speech which led me to rebel one year in my mid-twenties. I decided to stay at home with my then boyfriend and in true bohemian style we cooked a leg of lamb and sat by the fire eating just lamb and drinking wine. No walk, no speech, no church, heaven!

But I have had some great Christmases. Grandpa Robert's festivities were a whole lot of fun even for the adults. All of James' family would gather – brothers, other halves and children, and all thirteen of us would celebrate around his enormous dining table. There were always plenty of crackers and streamers and excessive amounts of food and laughter followed by endless silly board games played well into the night.

It was usually left to the guests to prepare and cook the meal with strict instructions. Robert was not inclined to eat his vegetables the slightest bit *al dente* and the poor unsuspecting carrots and sprouts had to be boiled within an inch of their lives. Still, what is Christmas without the humble sprout, soggy or otherwise?

As a child I always hoped it would snow on Christmas Day as it was extra magical. It rarely if ever did and certainly not in places like The Northern Territory of Australia. December was their wet season and I can clearly remember wading over to a neighbour's house on Boxing Day 1973. That year my parents had tantalisingly placed a large, heavy, beautifully wrapped box under the tree with my name on it. For days my imagination could hardly contain the excitement of what it might hold. When the day came to finally open it I savoured the moment by opening all my other presents first. But when I did open the packaging I was heartbroken to discover nothing more than a few old study books belonging to my father. My dismay was more than matched by my parents' hilarity at their joke. They had in fact bought me a guitar which had been hidden in a wardrobe and the box was nothing more than a distraction. Whilst I was very pleased with the guitar, somehow the disappointment of the box has never been forgotten.

This Christmas as with previous ones we shall have the annual ritual of naming the turkey. Everyone chooses a name which goes in a bag to be pulled when the turkey is dressed and ready to do the honourable thing and hop in the oven. Last year it was Ermintrude. Who knows what Christmas holds this year, but I do know that I will share it with Nigel and James, the children and Crumble and we will all have a wonderful day. It may not be a conventional family arrangement but it works and why go looking for the straw that breaks the camel's back when our house is made of bricks?

CHAPTER 33

THE FINAL STRAW

"Do you want a receipt?"

This had to be a joke – a John McEnroe, 'you cannot be serious' moment. The woman behind the till had already subjected me to the 'Do you want a bag?' routine. And just to prove that I am not an obsessive bag collector, I had politely declined the generous offer, even though my purchase – a bottle of wine – wouldn't fit into my beloved bumbag.

But having made my bag sacrifice I now had to justify the need for a till receipt. Call me an old fashioned ex-banker if you will but *yes*, I do expect to be given a receipt. Why not? It provides proof of purchase *and* I can keep an eye on the finances. Surely I can't be the only person on the planet who checks their receipts off against their bank statements each month? Do you?

Anyway, I had only just managed to save my receipt from her sweaty grip of disapproval before she was demanding to know if the next customer needed a bag. God forbid!

Call me cynical but I wonder if sometime in the future I attempt to buy anything, I will be asked if I actually need the purchases at all. Perhaps I could just put the whole lot back on the shelves and *voilà* – no bag or receipt required. Problem solved!

You probably think I have become bag-deranged. Not at all. I have bags of common sense though. After all, it's not as if I waste the bags and just throw them away. They are lovingly re-used as bin liners and let's face it, if I didn't, I would have to buy them.

Years ago in my banking days, I used to frequent my local drycleaners on a regular basis with work suits. The foreign woman who ran the business was always enthusiastic with her bag allocation if a little limited with social graces. "You wanna it in a baaag?" was pretty much all she ever said. Why anyone would want a bag when the clothes were already wrapped in cellophane on coat hangers I have no idea. Perhaps I should have accepted every bag opportunity presented to me and saved them for the rainy days when you don't know where your next bag is coming from.

Not that I have spent any time dwelling on my inability to afford the latest designer bag as my bumbag remains my faithful friend. However, it was not always so.

During my rental days in Finsbury Park, London, I owned a black handbag which was pretty ordinary and hardly likely to attract attention. Probably just as well, as it was a rough area in the 1980s. Ironically this very bag was targeted twice by muggers. One Friday night I returned home from the pub which I had gone to straight from work with banking colleagues. I was also fairly laden down with food shopping and only twenty feet from my front door when I was attacked. OMG! My handbag was snatched from my shoulder and the shopping bags literally ripped from my hands as I was knocked to the floor. Whilst not badly hurt – my knees were all grazed and my forehead cut – I was very shaken by the experience. My handbag I discovered discarded some way down the road emptied of its contents. Even the mugger could tell in his haste this was not a bag worthy of retention. The handbag I could not have cared less about but I was furious to have all my food bags stolen.

A couple of years later, living in a different part of London, I was mugged carrying the same old undesirable bag, coincidentally twenty feet from home again. This time, however, I screamed with rage at the injustice and gave chase much to my young attacker's surprise. I didn't catch him but I did get my bag back.

Two weeks later I had a phone call at work from a stranger saying they had found my bag in a park on the other side of London. The bag was kindly dropped off at the reception desk and unbelievably all the contents including my credit cards, a number of cheque books and a designer jumper were all intact. Only the cash was missing and that was minimal. Amazing but true.

Much like this book and despite all my ups and downs, I believe I have escaped without too much emotional baggage. And so I look forward to the next fifty years and everything life may throw at me. Whatever happens, I will continue to smile, look on the bright side and never forget that life's a bag of laughs.